Eboracus

Great and Grave Questions for American Politicians

With a Topic for American's Statesmen

Eboracus

Great and Grave Questions for American Politicians
With a Topic for American's Statesmen

ISBN/EAN: 9783337133498

Printed in Europe, USA, Canada, Australia, Japan

Cover: Foto ©Suzi / pixelio.de

More available books at **www.hansebooks.com**

Great and Grave Questions

FOR

AMERICAN POLITICIANS,

WITH A

TOPIC FOR AMERICA'S STATESMEN.

By EBORACUS.

"I owe a *paramount* allegiance to the whole Union—a subordinate one to my own State."—HENRY CLAY.

"*Free labor*, the acknowledged source of National wealth, is the bulwark of *free* institutions."—HON. WM. M. STEWART.

"Whilst, in the Old World, all physical labor is considered ungentleman-like, in America, on the contrary, not to work is looked upon as thoroughly degrading."—PULSKY.

"L'unite c'est la vie d'un peuple."—VICTOR HUGO.

"Abandon, *at once* and *for ever*, all notions of Secession, Nullification, and Disunion. Determine to live, and teach your children to live, as true American Citizens. There will be in the future, if there is not now, as much of pride and grandeur in the name of 'American Citizens,' as there once was in that of 'Roman Citizens.' The Republic is destined to go on increasing in National power and greatness for centuries to come."—B. F. PERRY, *Prov. Gov. of South Carolina.—Speech at Greenville, July 3d, 1865.*

BOSTON:

WALKER, FULLER & Co., 245 Washington street; A. WILLIAMS & Co., 100 Washington street.

CINCINNATI:

ROBERT CLARKE & Co., 55 West Fourth street.

New York:

C. S. WESTCOTT & CO.'S UNION PRINTING-HOUSE,

NO. 79 JOHN STREET.

1865.

TO THOSE WHO GAVE

Their Friendship

(UNASKED)

TO A STRANGER,

THESE PAGES ARE DEDICATED.

TABLE OF CONTENTS.

APPENDICES.

GREAT AND GRAVE QUESTIONS.

" The school of pain is hard but productive."—W. H. DIXON.

" It was only with the revolt against England that freedom came to any part of the black race in America."—W. H. DIXON.

> " Thy best Hope where, dear Liberty ?
> In fast upwinging time.
> Thy *first* strength where, proud Liberty ?
> In thine oppressor's crime."

" The end of the war has been obtained. The republic has fulfilled its destiny. Slavery, the plague-spot upon the fair body of our country, is dead, and no trumpet, though it were an angel's, can awake it to resurrection."—*Four Years in Secessia.*

" L'unité de l'homme correspond à l'unité de Dieu."—VICTOR HUGO.

> " Behold the few who stalk abroad in pride,
> In gilded trappings or a garb of gray,
> With haughty mien and soldierly disguise.
> They left our legislative halls, unstained
> Except by their offences in times past,
> And secretly in conclave met and swore,
> With all the hate of aristocracy,
> To make of the plebeians all—the poor,
> Degraded menials, subject to themselves ;
> And vowed, this end to gain they would destroy
> The happiest nation on the verdant earth.
> They talk of rights, but are the foes of God,
> Of man, and man's most dear-bought liberty.
> Nor have they more exalted aim in life

Than crushing right and revelling in wrong ;
Brigands, and pirates, vampires, blood they crave,
The fulsome, self-styled chivalry are they,
Who took the sword, by it to fall, indeed."

J. C. WEBSTER's Foe Unmasked.

UNSUCCESSFUL Revolutions and Rebellions are always beneficial to the progress of humanity.   The advantages are not
invariably immediate.   Sometimes they are very remote.
Only the profound and highly sensitive mind can penetrate
the confusion and blindness of incensed passions to see Law
and Progress.   Wealth, energy, intellect, blood — are not
wasted.   There may be mourning and weeping in the household over the sacrifice of a loved one—harassing poverty and
grim destitution may depose the queen of beauty enthroned
in luxury—intellect may exhaust its depths in devising plans
that are futile or inoperative—energy may droop piteously
and pitifully, broken-hearted at the loss of once giant
strength and inflexible determination—wealth may vanish
from workshops, warehouses, banks—nevertheless, in the
midst of seeming despair and ruin, the elements of Good are
silently but surely gathering and combining, the subtle
operations of Spiritual chemistry are evolving conditions and
forces that will everlastingly improve and bless mankind.
" God moves in a mysterious way ;" but the way is only
mysterious to the ignorant and the faithless—and to the
" worldly-wise," who scheme for solitary aggrandizement.

One Revolution and two Rebellions have convulsed opinions
and startled theorists on two continents.   The revolutionists
and rebellionists were defeated.   Many lamented the bitter
strifes.   Curious and " dry-as-dust" statisticians figured-up
the stupendous loss of life and property.   So many persons
shot—guillotined—so much wealth consumed unproductive-
ly.   The statisticians lay down their pens and fulminate

against the people for not practising business habits, and for not possessing mathematical knowledge ! Animate those figures with the soul of faith and the reckoners will see a magnificent compound interest — capital (blood shed and wealth scattered) yearly trebling itself in extending freedom, increasing knowledge, and deepening the faith of peoples in God's never-ceasing goodness.

The Restoration soon followed the death of CROMWELL. A selfish, heartless debauchee disgraced royalty and degraded his country. To enable him to satisfy his licentious extravagance, he accepted money from France. He transformed palaces into brothels, his court into a moral cesspool. The gentle sweetness of MILTON, that had mellowed and hallowed the stern councils of.the Puritans, had departed to a—garret or to Heaven. The grand far-seeing of CROMWELL was shrouded in death. The malicious execrations of cowards, fools, hypocrites, and knaves, brayed in vain over the unoccupied clay-tenement. The psalms and Scripture-comfort sung and given to each other by pale women and disappointed men, were invoked and sought in dark recesses. The good and noble mourned the national gyrations of moral dissolution. The vile herds who fattened on political corruption, and gloated over royal depravity, danced gleefully amid the ruins of a nation's glory. Not so ! The ruins were not of glory, but of sin. Fiends were dancing amid the wreck of despotism. The flames of hell lighted the terrible scene. The slowly-burning embers of Absolutism were fitfully gleaming around the hiding-places of wise patriots who were breathing fervent prayers to CHRIST. God was operating for the nation's benefit—for the world's advancement. But the people did not *then* see what we now *know*. In clouds of smoke, where steel was clashing, Progress was nestling and growing serenely and securely as an infant in its mother's arms.

The first French Revolution violently estranged men from each other in all modern nations. It appalled BURKE, but pleased the operatives of England. France became, as many supposed and asserted, a chaos of bloody crimes. The wit of VOLTAIRE, the eloquence of DE HOLBACH, the startling logic of the CURE MESLIER, the well-aimed shafts of DIDEROT, had shattered priestly power and torn-up the roots of a noble Christian faith. ROUSSEAU had shattered the political edifice. The sickly and nervous man, weak as a child and fearful as a maniac, had hurled thunderbolts against the proud monarchy, and split the gorgeous throne asunder. What a rushing to-and-fro of priestly apes and political imbeciles! The sky lurid, the atmosphere dark and sultry, the waters roaring and rushing, oratorical giants grappling with each other, "Clubs" declaiming against old while evolving and explaining new theories, mobs starving and execrating—the nobility scattered, flying, gasping for a foreign shore—and, in the midst of this Pandemonium of passions, vanities, ambitions and deadly antagonisms, the Guillotine cast its revolting but purging shadow of an impartial Nemesis.

In time, the grim strife merged into the Consulate and the Empire—the Empire vanished before Monarchy uplifted on bayonets—and, again, Monarchy fled, as once more the Empire stealthily (having lost its martial boldness) advanced.

Was the Revolution useless? Was the land soddened with blood in vain? Did rival "patriots" depose each other in an objectless tragedy? Keenly examine the history of France during the past three centuries, cast your eyes over the partially cleared ground, and the answer will not be affirmative nor uncertain. MACKINTOSH vindicates the Revolution, and BUCKLE displays his learning and acumen in giving proof of the blessings showered on the pathway of Civilization by those who cut the locks of strength of the Samson of Absolutism. The Bastile, and nearly all it represented, has vanished into thin air. Imbeciles cannot again occupy the palaces of France, though scheming, crafty, subtle hypocrites may. BERANGER is enthroned in the sentiments of the French people, and the psalm of eloquence for freedom is poured-forth in never-ceasing strains by VICTOR HUGO—the soul and harp of France. The sallow-faced monster of Imperialism is obliged to use the rhetoric of progress and mouthe the syllogisms of freedom.

Northern resistance to the Southern Rebellion was a ghost as horrible to the nations as was the French Revolution. The manners of the times of PITT have been adopted in England in treating of the American struggle. The same absurdities of language, rashness of theories, violence of denunciation, pomposity of judgments, have been repeated. The intellect and patriotism of England throbbing for the North—the ignorance, passions, prejudice, and greed, yelling for the South. Profound philosophy, the lessons of history and the dignity of truth, marshalled for the North—reckless lying, audacious brutishness, the bitterness of vulgar cunning, plotting for the South. In the House of Commons the same pleasing and revolting features are seen. The oratory of BRIGHT, the energy of TAYLOR, the experience of FOSTER, overruling the ignorant petulance of ROEBUCK, the impudence of LAIRD, and the stupidity of GREGORY.

The Great Rebellion of England struggled for freedom, the contending parties in France during the Revolution were *all* opposed to despotism, and strove for liberty according to the measure of their understandings. The Southern Rebellion was instituted to overthrow freedom and progress. Its leading men hated free schools, free speech, free press, free thinking—they only loved slavery, subordination, and despotic government. They resolved that no " law denying or impairing the *right* of PROPERTY in negro slaves shall be passed." The long screech of South Carolina against the North was on behalf of retrogression, moral desolation, Heathenism, and national destruction. Thirty millions of human beings were driven to shed each other's blood to satisfy the dark and remorseless designs of a clique of infernal sinners. The rich harvests of industry were destroyed by political barbarians. Dissolute crusaders against Civilization crawled round the mountains, tainted the once delightful atmosphere with moral poison, and darkened the Heavens with the breath of destruction. The bright and gentle feathered denizens of the air, the forests, and the valleys, were scared by new and dismal sounds. The pioneer was arrested in his pilgrimage through the wilds to extend human progress—his unblunted axe was no longer required. The soft, sweet music of murmuring streams and gentle zephyrs, was hushed in the thunders of cannon and the groans of dying demons and patriots. Black hearts raging and shedding blood for black purposes. The stars veiled in the smoke of rebellion, the air filled with the moans of the bleeding and the sobs of the bereaved. But Progress was in the midst—for over all God reigneth.

"You can never conquer the South," was the hourly-proclaimed words of knaves and imbeciles, here and abroad, " therefore, stop the unholy war." " The North may make a Poland of the South," said LORD CAMPBELL, " but it cannot be conquered ;" and, while he was speaking in Manchester, the war-steeds of freedom dashed over the serried hosts of Devildom ! The North has Triumphed — rebellion *for* slavery is crushed—and Civilization is preparing to march through the world under the bright banner of American Republicanism.

From the smouldering embers of camp fires—amid the wreck of cities and the pauperism of once gay homes—amid mountains tinged with blood and the bankruptcy of Southern credit—amid the loneliness of little orphans and the tortures of wives divorced from wedded love by the Furies of war—amid the groves of a sunny land turned into a reeking burial-ground—emerges the sable forms (of young and old, of strong and feeble, of the growing and the decaying) of FOUR MILLIONS emancipated from the "new empire" built out of the quarried materials from the infernal regions. Manacles struck off from the gored limbs of slaves by a— Proclamation, "done at the City of Washington, this first day of January, in the year of our Lord one thousand eight hundred and sixty-three, and of the Independence of the United States the eighty-seventh." Once more, blood, wealth, energy, have produced an abundant harvest—*freedom !* Revolutions and Rebellions, apparently unsuccessful, are not failures but instruments—are not horrors but blessings—are not the Devil's luxuries, but God's unerring means of bringing man back to the Garden of Eden. Every tear shed in times of civil war is a jewel dropped into the diadem of universal Civilization. Every heart's throb hushed on gory plains is the arranging of elements that will fill the valleys of National life with harmonious forms, ever emitting sweet perfume and rich odors that blend with a purified atmosphere, where the Psalms of Freedom are everlastingly trilled-forth amidst Beauty and Clearness—amidst Spiritual Beauty and Moral Clearness. O God ! we adore Thee for this second rebellion—this Southern scourge, but greater blessing.

" Let men do wrong upon system, and they will soon imbibe a passion to do wrong—and a passion to do wrong in one form, has a natural affinity with propensities to do so in other forms."—R. VAUGHAN, D. D.

" One of the Southern leaders, speaking about the institution, said, in 1849 : 'If left to the tender mercies of the Federal Government, its fate is doomed. With the prejudice of the age against it, it requires for its kind development a fostering government over it. It could scarcely subsist without its protection!' "

" The Democratic party sympathizes with us, and some of its influential leaders are pledged to our side. They will sow division there [in the North], and paralyze the Free States."—*Among the Pines.*

" Education the criterion of the right of suffrage, not property. I do not believe in a government of ignorance, whether by the rich, or poor, the many or the few."—HON. R. J. WALKER.

After emancipating the slaves, the next great good coming from the Southern Rebellion is the breaking-up of the old political cliques and parties. The Woolly-Heads, the Whigs,* the Silver-Greys, the Know-Nothings, the Barn-

---

* " Yer an Abolisherner, aint ye ?"
" No ; I'm an old-fashioned Whig."
" What's that ? Never heerd on them afore."
" An old-fashioned Whig, madam, is a man whose political principles are perfect, and who is as perfect as his principles."
That was a " stumper " for the poor woman, who evidently did not understand one half of the sentence.
" Right sort of folks, them," she said, in a half-inquiring tone.
" YES; BUT THEY'RE ALL DEAD NOW."—*Among the Pines.*

Burners, the Free Democrats, are all *non est*. The great Democratic party is shattered—the party that in Baltimore, in June, 1852—

" *Resolved*, That the Democratic party will resist *all* attempts at renewing in Congress, or out of it, the agitation of the Slavery question, under whatever shape or color the attempt may be made."

The great Democratic party that assisted Southern slave-mongers to become all-powerful in Congress and the creators of Presidents, is shivered. When PULSKY was in America in 1852, he declared that—

" No President can be nominated or elected without the concurrence of the Southern States; no statesman, therefore, who does not share the opinions of the South, can ever aspire to the highest post in the Union, whatever might be otherwise his statesmanship or his talents; though the population of the Free States amount to thirteen millions, and that of the whites in the South only to six millions."

That great Democratic party that supported Southern bullies to frighten, intimidate, and coerce, must be *converted* or annihilated. When in power, the Southerners demoralized their country and bullied the world. The latter fact was not forgotten when the revolting Confederacy went begging, imploring, and beseeching to Europe. RUSSELL jogged the memory of the South in the following paragraph :

" The people in the seceding States, aware in their consciences that they have been most active in their hostility to Great Britain, and whilst they were in power were *mainly* responsible for the defiant, irritating, and insulting tone commonly used to us by American statesmen, are anxious at the present moment, when so much depends on the action of foreign countries, to remove unfavorable impressions from our minds by declarations of good-will, respect, and admiration, not quite compatible with the language of their leaders in times not long gone by."

The Democratic party has supported the foes of intellect and the friends of ignorance. Take a solitary but significant fact from the history of the rule of the slave-oligarchy in the South. Here it is—

" In a population of 524,000 freemen, there are 41,000 white adults in Georgia (in 1852) who cannot read, and the number of children, whose parents are not able to send them to school, is upwards of 38,000."

It should, also, be remembered, that in the State named, the Old Dominion, in " 1677, no printing-press was *allowed* in Virginia." A royal governor had previously (in 1671) said, " I thank God, there are no free schools and no printing ; and I hope we shall not have these hundred years." On this revolting desire by a royal barbarian, W. P. ATKINSON pertinently remarks—" The present condition of that State (Virginia) is a striking commentary on the sentiment."*

The ruling passion of the South for repression of opinion and despotism was strong in the hour of death, for a traveller down South during the death-rattle, says :

" Charges of abolitionism appear in the reports of police cases in the papers every morning ; and persons found guilty, not of expressing opinions against slavery, but of stating their belief that the Northerners will be successful, are sent to prison for six months."

The same writer says :

" In the South, the press threatened me with tar and feathers, because I did not see the beauties of their domestic institution."

Can the foreign traveller expect any other treatment from men whose stolid hearts and ruthless brains were impervious to the solvent influence of the sufferings and tears of little

---

* *Classical and Scientific Studies.* Pub. by SEVER & FRANCIS, Cambridge, Massachusetts.

children ! Read this affecting incident that affected not Southern society :

" The little negroes who ran about were smart, but some of them came into violent collision, and were cuffed incontinently. One mild-looking little fellow stood by my side and appeared so sad that I asked him, ' Are you happy, my boy ?' He looked quite frightened. ' Why don't you answer me?' ' I'se afeered, sir ; I can't tell that to massa.' ' Is not your master kind to you ?' ' Massa very kind man, sir ; very good man when he is not angry with me,' and his eyes filled with tears to the brim."

The South is very good when not angry with freedom, knowledge, and progress ! But when has it not been angry with these angels of the earth ?

The Democratic party has countenanced and supported debt-repudiating scoundrels. JEFF. DAVIS grinned at the losses of the confiding who had lent their money to the State of Mississippi, and termed their tears "crocodile." The Confederacy was based on repudiation—repudiation of principles, of freedom, morality, and debt. At the commencement of the war, the Special Correspondent of *The Times* (London), was obliged to declare—

"The North has set out with the principle of paying for everything, the South with the principle of paying for nothing."

The Democratic party has supported the degraders of public sentiment and the debasers of public opinion. The historian says :

" The tone of public feeling in the United States has retrograded in the course of a couple of generations."—J. M. LUDLOW's *Hist. of United States*.

In characterizing the tendency and tone of society in Mississippi, from 1840 to 1860, the HON. R. J. WALKER uses these words : " The incredible extent to which the public sentiment of that day was debased "—" the moral waste and desolation of that dreadful period." Shall we be surprised, when even the " high-blood " of Virginia poured from the fountains of English crime. Read—

" Nor must we forget, as a set-off to the high blood of which Virginia boasts, that that Colony was for a length of time a place of penal transportation."

After such depressing recitals, it is refreshing to be told that—

" The legislature of Massachusetts passed a Bill which practically defeated the surrender of fugitive slaves, and this step had been *followed* by Connecticut and Vermont."

Ah ! those horrible New England States, they are not the garden of liberty—they are full of " insult and wrong," and they work " with the energy of devils incarnate to make the world believe their absurd statements." So says *Anti-Abolition Tracts*, No. 1.

The Democratic party has tenaciously supported the enemies of well-paid labor. Africans were brought to America so that labor could be effectually and for ever capitalized. White men wanted to become rich out of the degradation of black men, women, and children. The desire was " mean," the act was barbarous. On this important topic we will cull a few facts from history. DR. ROBERTSON informs us (*Hist. of America*) that—

" As early as the year 1503, a few negro slaves had been sent into the New World. In the year 1511, FERDINAND permitted the importation of them in greater numbers. They are found to be a more robust and hardy race than the natives of America. They were more capable of enduring fatigue, more *patient* under servitude, and the labor of *one negro* was computed to be equal to that of four Indians."

The docility and strength of the negro made him an easy prey for the greed and tyranny of Godless men. Not always is the literal reason assigned for making the negro a slave. In the following passage a climatorial reason is assigned for covering an infamous wrong. We quote from MARY HOW-ITT'S work (*Hist. of America*)—

" GOVERNOR YEAMANS introduced negro slavery (into South Carolina), bringing with him a cargo of slaves from Barbadoes. The *heat* of the climate rendering labor very difficult to the whites, and from its first settlement, South Carolina was a slave state.

" The climate of South Carolina was not only *congenial* to the negro, but the temper of the people made them willingly avail themselves of slave labor—and very soon the slave population far outnumbered the whites."

This passage is open to merry criticism, but our space is too limited for us to indulge in the luxury. But what has slavery done for South Carolina ? The Hungarian traveller thus answers :

" The plantations in South Carolina, along the railway, seemed much poorer than in any other part of the South we had visited, and the cabins of the negroes looked little better than kennels."

This observer wrote in 1852, and in 1860 RUSSELL thus described the negro kennels :

" The huts stand in a row, like a street, each detached, with a pantry house of rude planks behind it. No attempt at any drainage or any convenience existed near them, and the same remark applies to very good houses of white people in the South. Heaps of oyster-shells, broken crockery, old shoes, rags, and feathers, were found near each hut. The huts were all alike windowless, and the apertures, intended to be glazed some fine day, were generally filled up with a deal board. The roofs were shingle, and the whitewash, which had once given the settlement an air of cleanliness, was now only to be traced by patches which had escaped the action of the rain. I observed that many of the doors were fastened by a padlock and chain outside."

The atrocious cruelty practised in South Carolina for the maintenance of accursed slavery is related in the Appendix. We now turn to the opposition to and final adoption of slavery in Georgia. The founder of Georgia was a brave and God-fearing man. He affirmed that "slavery was contrary to the Gospel, as well as to the fundamental law of England. We will not permit a law which allows such horrid crimes." The early religious conscience of Georgia resisted the adoption of slavery.

" The Moravians opposed slavery as contrary to the Gospel. . . . . Slaves were at first hired from Carolina for a short period or during life, and a sum equal to the value of the slave paid in advance. Thus, by degrees, Georgia became a planting state, with slave-labor, like Carolina."— MARY HOWITT's *Hist. of America.*

American authors declare that "idlers and enemies of the industrious whites" transformed Georgia into a slave state. We quote the following passage by T. S. ARTHUR and W. H. CARPENTER :

" But evil counsel prevailed. The idlers far outnumbered those who worked, and although the trustees stood out for a long time, slaves were eventually admitted, and the energies of the industrious whites correspondingly paralyzed."—LIPPINCOTT's *Histories, Georgia.*

Another able writer (GOODELL) insists that—

" The first introduction of slaves into Georgia was in direct violation of express statutes of the colony itself, until slaveholders gained the ascendency and repealed the laws. Into the other Colonies slaves were introduced a long time before there were any Colonial enactments authorizing it, and consequently any show of legal sanction."

These facts, and the revolting influence of these facts, are supported by the Democratic party. Will workingmen, will Americans, continue to countenance this party, unless it speedily changes the objects of its affections? In Mary-land—

" Black slaves, as being *cheaper*, were preferred to white laborers ; an act, therefore, was passed in 1671, for encouraging the importation of ne-groes, which, in consequence of the intercepted trade with Holland, had almost ceased."

To make men constantly drudge, to make them do so *cheaply*, are primary objects of the slave-mongers. Listen to one of slavery's admirers, who unblushingly declares that—

" The *coercion* of slavery *alone* is adequate to form man to habits of *labor*. Without it there can be no accumulation of property, no provi-dence for the future, no taste for comforts, which are the characteristics of Civilization."

Here is a solitary sample of the " comforts " that *colored* laborers have bestowed upon them :

" *All* that a slave possesses belongs to his master, he possesses nothing of his own except *peculium ;* that is to say, the sum of money or moveable estate which his master chooses he shall possess."—*Civil Code of Louisi-ana*.

The slave must not have any of the fruits of his industry, the master alone must have the whole of the *golden* harvest. How unlike the motive that induced PRINCE HENRY to order negroes into slavery. *He* did so for the supposed benefit of the enslaved, not to feed the greedy savageness of white men. The fact is worth repeating in this century of demoralized party politics :

" PRINCE HENRY of Portugal orders that if GONCALVERT should not be able to obtain so many negroes (as had been mentioned) in exchange for the three Moors, yet that he should take them ; for whatever number he should get, he should gain souls, because they (the negroes) might be *con-*

verted to the faith, which could not be managed with the Moors."—*Conq. of the New World.*

The negroes' conversion from Heathenism to Christianity did not improve their temporal condition in South Carolina. An extract from the Code of South Carolina proves this assertion. Will the reader carefully peruse this horrible paragraph ? :

" And it is hereby declared *lawful* for any negro, or Indian slave, or *any other* slave or slaves whatever, to receive and profess the Christian faith, and to be thereunto baptized; but *notwithstanding* such slave or slaves shall receive or profess the Christian religion and be baptized, he or they *shall not* be manumitted."

The Democratic party has enabled the South to consolidate and extend slavery. It has made the United States a nursery of abominations. It has reproduced Heathenism in the modern world. It has, for a time, fastened Heathenism on a continent that should be devoted to Christianity. On what other spot could Heathenism have taken fresh root, and exerted renewed energy ? A profound thinker shall give the summing-up of evidence in answer to this question—

"Had not America afforded a market for slaves, we hardly see where else it could have grown up, and if it had not grown up there, legitimate commerce would have come in its place, and prevented any such trade. Black slaves might have been for some time a favorite part of the grandeur of a great household, but we do not see how they could have occupied a country already stocked with hardy laborers fitted for the soil, as was the case with Europe."

And here we end this section of our work.

"Thy birthplace where, young Liberty?
In graves 'neath heroes' ashes.
Thy dwelling, where, sweet Liberty?
In hearts, where free blood dashes."

The old party political terms must cease, sectional politics must disappear. Political rivalry produces jealousy, and jealousy begets strife. The monarchies of Europe did not become strong until provinces, counties, and cities, became consolidated into nations. The theological Provincialisms of France deluged her with blood. The county-quarrels of England covered her broad acres with anarchy. The fierce contentions of Ireland made her an easy prey to the invader. The bitter hatreds of opposing Poles, palsied the power of Poland, and made her a miserable wreck. The vanities and enmities of the Greek republics broke the spell of the noblest minds, and covered a fair region with broken monuments, amid which the scholars of all times lament, and patriots mourn. It is the thought, the sentiment, the aspiration of Nationality that make a people grow in strength, extend in knowledge, and increase in grandeur. It is an ardent love for country (not "sections") that makes the family a home of patriotic felicity. The cry for unity of parts is a psalm set to divine music. Under the dome of a nation, WASHINGTON becomes the type of a people—within the precincts of a section, he becomes a governor, representing local littleness.

2

To produce a nation there must be principles, sentiment, and aspiration—and a political nomenclature that does not degrade principles into expedients, nor sentiment into anarchy, nor aspiration into mere materialism. The principles must result from wisdom grounded in virtue, the sentiment must arise from affectionate enthusiasm, and the aspiration must be produced by Christian culture. Under such conditions, a people will become a nation, and the nation will become a moral and industrial power. No better illustrations could be cited of the soundness of the above statements than the condition of the Southern and Northern States. In spite of many deviations, the Northern States have steadily moved in the orbit of morality, industry, and prosperity—morality graced with religion, industry sanctified with philanthropy, and prosperity preserved for the world's advantage and progress. Without deviations, the Southern States have wildly marched to absolutism, degradation, and limitation of power.* The North has tended to unity, the South to

---

* These assertions are verified by facts gathered by English travellers and historians. In CHAMBER's work on *American Slavery and Color*, we read—" At the opening of the Revolutionary war, there were slaves in al the revolted Colonies; even in Massachusetts, the land of the 'Pilgrim Fathers,' there were slaves, and sales of slaves, too; though it is proper to add, that Massachusetts was the *first* to set the example of passing an act of general emancipation." But, at the same time, what was the South doing? MARY HOWITT will give the answer. She says: " The same year (1712) that Massachusetts passed her prohibitory law, South Carolina enacted her *first* slave law." (See *Hist. of America*.) And the following relation, by the same historian, shows that the North has steadily but firmly advanced while the South was receding into complete barbarism: "When the Constitution of the United States was passed, in 1789, the slave-trade was formally prohibited after the year 1808, and it was generally assumed that the emancipation of the Africans in America would take place in a short space of time through voluntary manumissions by the slave-owners themselves. But it was acknowledged that they needed some time for so managing their affairs that a sudden transition might not endanger their economical welfare. WASHINGTON himself held this opinion, and proved his desires practically by freeing his slaves in his last

anarchy. The North has opened-up her resources, the South has gradually buried her treasures in the grave of ignorance. It is not necessary to prolong the references, the facts stare upon us like the eyes of a basilisk! The results produced in the North and emerging in the West, must be realized *all over* the continent. No withered leaves should be permitted to shade the beauty of a stately tree. No storms must wash away the sweets from Flora's perfumed lips. No cloud must veil the harvest moon from gleesome husbandmen. No discordant note should mar the softness of a lover's melody. One hope, one faith, one destiny, must be the watchwords of Americans—and a nation, a people, an example, must be the thrilling echoes.

Sectional terms will have to be abandoned, sectional notions will have to be denounced. Words that sound-forth National thought, sentiment, and aspiration, will have to be the language of the future of this people. Materialistic absolutists, who "cant" with theology and blaspheme religion with shallow hypocrisy, must never again be permitted to disgrace Congress and degrade the country. The young Hercules of freedom should rise from his cradle of indifference and *crush* the serpents. Oh! what multitudes on dis-

---

will." A few more facts may be cited with advantage: "Indiana and Illinois have a series of Black Laws, which deprive the Negro of political privileges and the validity of his oath. Ohio repealed her Black Laws a few years ago. In Iowa, Michigan, Pennsylvania, and Connecticut, Negroes were deprived of political privileges. In New York, Negroes can vote if they have real estate of the value of $250. In New England States (except Connecticut), Negro votes are equal to the whites. In Massachusetts, Negroes are eligible to the highest offices." "Slavery was abolished in New York in 1825; but in New Jersey, Rhode Island, and Connecticut, not till 1850." And as a proof of advance, *real* advancement in the North, and of dismal receding into barbarism in the South, note this astounding fact: "The churches in New York equal in value *all* the churches in all the fifteen Slave States."

tant shores will rejoice when the deed is done. The air will resound with the plaudits of up-risen pauperism and unfettered energies.

To have a healthy human being, there must be perfect freedom of function of each part or organ. To have a nation, there must be absolute freedom for each adult member of the population. Freedom, not license, for *each one*, not solely for one hundred or one million—to the terribly disgraceful exclusion of the rest of the community. Each son of God must be, or should be, a man on earth, not a slave, for "if slavery is not wrong, nothing is wrong." Each son of God should be a man, not a tyrant, not an isolated monster draped in the splendor of infamy, whose music is the groans of the oppressed and the curses of the poor. And no pretext, no pretence, no shuffle, no subterfuge, should be permitted to prevent an organ or man from fulfilling its or his function. Let not one man usurp the functions of another man. Let not one man think, and feel, and aspire for another—let each man think, feel, and aspire for himself.

"Life, liberty, and the pursuit of happiness," are conditions of existence. Unless we exercise those functions, we become diseased, a part of our body-politic perishes. It is liberty that makes the life of a man, and life should be strong enough to guard and maintain liberty. The pursuit of happiness flows from freedom of action. When a government or monarchy regulates the volition of a people, an outrageous presumption is committed, and desolating oppression is enforced. The country where such is done, stagnates, the people become mere machines, and madness or inanity becomes the living death of the multitude. The child thrives only when allowed to talk and to play. When its voluble questions are a prattle about mysteries that philosophers cannot penetrate—when it romps and shouts, jumps and roars, flings toys about and breaks the dear-bought crockery—how very happy is the daring creature, how its whole forces are rapidly developing into proportions that will make the man of bravery and wisdom ! But chill the little thing into silence, forbid its wild antics, hush its merry shouts of budding joys—and what a wretched, shrinking, withering, passionless, stunted mass of adult imbecility the creature will become. The seed-germ must be free to put-forth and enlarge the area of its root-fibres, or it will die, or become deformed in its developments, and *that* is partial death. But let the seed-germ have freedom and space, and it will become useful and beautiful. It is liberty, dear liberty, that giveth the increase. It is liberty that makes clouds and skies alike captivating to the free. It is liberty that tills the rocky ground, and covers the seas with argosies. It is liberty that increases knowledge, and makes the circles of fancy bright and manifold.

It is "life, liberty, and the pursuit of happiness," guaranteed to each individual that constitute a nation. Not the number of a population, not the vastness of mountains nor out-stretching plains, with uniformity of intellectual stagnation, that produce a nation—though they may make an empire of gilded iniquity. It is fecundent life revelling in liberty that transforms bodies into men, and men into nations. This fact is well stated by a Boston preacher, who, in charming eloquence, thus speaks :

" In estimating the value of a nation, you must not merely count the men, you must weigh them. You must not barely weigh the dollars, but gauge, and measure, and scan the quality of the men who own the dollars. An armful of Hebrews, a handful of old Greeks, have been of more value to the human race than all the four hundred millions of Chinese, with their Tartar and Malay progenitors. A single Moses, Socrates, or Jesus, would weigh down whole provinces of the Celestial Empire."

Just as Boston and Lowell "weigh down" the whole of the Southern States, though having a more generous soil, and greater material resources to bless the energy of man. Energy of man!   Down   South?   No! *Stagnation* of man, you mean—perishing of soil, you mean—darkening fair regions with the breath of ignorance, you mean.

Ignorance is the strength of a tyrant, but it is the pauperism of a people. Ignorance can only be dissipated by liberty.   Liberty is the instrument through which knowledge is obtained.   And every man must be free.   " This country, with its institutions, belongs to the people who inhabit it." Not to one man, not to one State, but "to the people." Who are the people?   Those " who inhabit it."   Whoever dares to dispute this position is a Heathen—the advocate of Paganism.   But are ignorant negroes to have liberty? Yes! liberty that is nestled in political power—and that power will, in time, protect them from ignorance.   We must be a nation, not of the dead and living chained together, as heretofore.   The dead are to be buried, and we are to be a nation all-alive, strong, and energetic.   Our only source of power, progress, and perpetuity, is to make of each male body a man in social life and political relations ; and to make of each female a woman of love, refinement, parental affection, National aspirations, and piety tinctured with toleration ; not to deprive us of brain-power, not to strangle intellectual activity.   An opponent to emancipation declares that " negroes withdrawn from the plantations are set to work ; among them there are excellent mechanics."   So skilled in slavery are many—what would the whole be in freedom ?

" Life, liberty, and the pursuit of happiness—that, to secure those rights, governments are instituted among men, *deriving* their just powers *from* the CONSENT *of the gov-*

erned." These explicit words are from the decalogue of our country. Here is Nationality emphatically enunciated. No reservation about color, no exclusion on the pretence of ignorance. This is to be the anchor of our State, if we are to continue as a State, a Nation, and not as a series of diverse fragments. All political questions that involve principles must be settled by a reference to the Declaration of Independence. This document proclaimed for us a Nation, and the right to be a nation was conquered for us by WASHINGTON. But political ruffianism trod on the Declaration, struck down those who were inspired by the principles of the Declaration, and, at last, caused our fair valleys to be reddened with the blood of the brave and the gentle. A second time we have won the right to be a nation—a second time the best of the people have shed their blood, and spent their treasures to be a nation. A second time the laurels deck the sword—a second time maimed heroes hobble through peace to their fathers' grave—a second time the prayers of the just have been answered—*and now* WE WILL, WE MUST be a Nation.

This country cannot be republics, like Greece. The Declaration and the Constitution alike forbid such structures on this continent. We can be only *a* republic, " one and indivisible." The States are not republics—they are only *parts* of a great whole. They came into the Union, after grave deliberation, to be parts of a nation. The origin of the Union is the very cradle of American Nationality. Divide the nation, and each section will have supposed interests to protect, and supposed wrongs to avenge. Has it not been so in the past? And shall it be so again? A third conflict would end disastrously, for the moral forces of the country would be weakened. An increased amount of indifference to principles and brutal selfishness would ensue. Even now, it will be long before the tinge of slavery will fade from the prejudices of a certain portion of our people. Custom is a tyrant not easily changed. The disastrous consequences flowing from division, supposed wrongs, and disregard of Unity and Nationality, were prophetically seen by WASHINGTON. His words cannot be too often presented to the community—hence, we reprint them here, for they form an excellent commentary on the Declaration and Constitution. The reader is urged to read them more than once.

"In contemplating the causes which may disturb our Union, it occurs, as matter of serious concern, that any ground should have been furnished for characterizing parties by *geographical* discriminations. *Northern* and *Southern, Atlantic* and *Western ;* whence designing men may endeavor to excite a belief, that there is a real difference of local interests and views. One of the expedients of party to acquire influence, within particular districts, is to misrepresent the opinions and aims of other districts. You cannot shield yourselves too much against the jealousies and heartburnings which spring from these misrepresentations; they tend to render alien to each other those who ought to be bound together by fraternal affection.

"To the efficacy and permanency of your Union, a Government for the whole is indispensable. No alliances, however strict, between the parts can be an adequate substitute ; they must inevitably experience the infractions and interruptions that all alliances in all times have experienced.

"The unity of Government constitutes you one people ; it is a main pillar in the edifice of your real independence, the support of your tranquillity at home, your peace abroad ; of your safety ; of your prosperity ; of that very LIBERTY which you so highly prize. But as it is easy to foresee, that, from different causes and from different quarters, much pains will be taken, many artifices employed, to weaken in your mind the conviction of this truth ; as this is the point in your political fortress against which the battering of internal and external enemies will be most constantly and actively (though often secretly and insidiously) directed, it is of infinite moment, that you should properly estimate the immense value of your national Union to your collective and individual happiness; that you should cherish a cordial, habitual, and immovable attachment to it ;

accustoming yourselves to think and speak of it as the palladium of your political safety and prosperity ; watching for its preservation with jealous anxiety ; discountenancing whatever may suggest even a suspicion, that it can in any event be abandoned ; and indignantly frowning upon the first dawning of every attempt to alienate any portion of our country from the rest, or to enfeeble the sacred ties which now link together the various parts."

Almost unnecessary seems the task of writing about Union and Nationality after these wise and earnest words of the first President of the United States. The lofty tone, the profound patriotism, the mournful solemnity of the exhortation, should be sufficient to imbue the people with a never-ceasing love for American nationality. On the sword of the first President is suspended the Proclamation of Emancipation by the Martyred President, *to save* the Union ! Freedom for white men through WASHINGTON— freedom for *all* men through LINCOLN ! And here, in closing this division of our labors, devoted to a great and grave theme, however imperfectly though lovingly entered upon— we resolve to

" do our duty in our shop, in our kitchen, the market, the street, the office, the school, the house, just as faithfully as if we stood in the front rank of some great battle, and we knew that victory for mankind depended on our bravery, strength, and skill. When we do that, the humblest of us will be serving in that great army which achieves the welfare of the world." *

---

* *Lessons from the World of Matter and the World of Man.* By T. PARKER. Boston : C. W. SLACK.

" The blessing of Almighty God will come down upon the noblest people the world ever saw—who have triumphed over Theocracy, Monarchy, Aristocracy, Despotocracy, and have got a Democracy—a government of all, for all, and by all—a Church without a Bishop, a State without a King, a Community without a Lord, and a family without a Slave."—T. PARKER.

" The blessed revolution is begun; but it must be carried forward, by officials and private citizens."—*The New York Times*, Aug. 2, 1865.

England and France have become nations through numerous internal conflicts. They have progressed through murder and rapine to Constitutions that have consolidated energies and concentrated power. A tendency to unity has graduated to fixity, and fixity has produced oneness—or, in other words, a people and peoples. The grand periods of England's greatness were under HENRY THE EIGHTH, QUEEN ELIZABETH, and the COMMONWEALTH—the grandest period *is now*, under QUEEN VICTORIA, because the feeble remains of despotism are being grasped by freedom to be hurled into oblivion. England's Magna Charta, Petition and Bill of Rights, and her Reform Bill, are stages in the process of forming a Constitution for freedom, equity, and progress. As England's children become more free, they become more active and more prosperous. The pauper-dullness of her agricultural counties gradually diminishes as freedom advances—and the fierce roughness of her manufacturing districts subsides as prosperity spreads over freedom's pathway.

And then the people become intensely national—proud of their being, because of their achievements. They boast—for they have done something—something creditable to themselves, and ennobling of mankind.

The American Colonies had no tendency to unity, had no conception of nationality. They could not, by their own internal volition, have become a nation. Their rival opinions, their rival politics (resulting from strange diversity of origin) prevented oneness of power. A common *outward* danger was needed to arouse to a sense of the necessity for common action through common organization. Despotism made active the Republican convictions of the Northern people, and made timorous the conduct of Southern lovers of monarchy and theological uniformity in ecclesiastical bonds. The irrevocable destiny that impelled Colonists and the mother-country to deadly strife, was the cradle of American nationality. Rocked in the cradle of political passions and social anomalies, the puny infant grew to have a Constitution of tolerable strength and vast recuperative forces. The Revolution transformed the Colonies into States, a transformation of significant importance—but the significancy of the wondrous change has not, that we are aware, been adequately dwelt on by either American or foreign writers, and no distinct book has been devoted to this precious subject in America's history and progress. Changing the Colonies into States was the inception of Nationality—it was a fruitful germ of astounding results, vitalized by war's fructiviousness—wisdom and disinterestedness had placed manifold glories and blessings in the cradle — intended for the future.

In political geography, the "shires" of England correspond to the states of America. Since 1832 in England and 1788–9 in America, how different has been the progress in the two countries in consolidating and methodizing national power! England's shires have been harmoniously arranged into parts of a nation—their municipal rights and privileges have been clearly defined in public opinion, in public sentiment, and calmly realized through a sense of public duty. In the States, the anarchy of political opinions and sentiments has caused confusion in internal arrangements, and an absence of completeness and perfection in the parts. Public usefulness, convenience, and comfort, have been sacrificed in the mad rage for sectional sovereignty. Everything has been projected and attempted, to be abandoned and left as wrecks of " good intentions." While ranting for sectional power and arrogance, the finely chiselling into the symmetry of a nation the massive rocks that were quarried by the sword and the cannon has been unwisely neglected—fragments of strength and beauty have been scattered in profuse confusion, shocking the appreciative and sensitive taste of the artistic, and annoying the prophetic insight of the patriot and the philosopher. It is harmony of arrangement that produces grandeur, and methodical action that produces irresistible dynamics. The ripening process of Nationality out of chaos cannot be effected by chaos of opinions and anarchy of sentiment. Order is strength—strength in a Nation is the product of harmony of parts.

To be a Citizen of America, not of a state, will have to be the proud prerogative of each man on this continent— if this Republic is to be (as indeed she ought, and God's mercies to her manifest that Heaven desires she should be) the Ark of free Civilization in future for the whole world. The vanities of states will have to be absorbed into the pride of being an American, inhabiting a land not cursed with sacerdotal robbery and the gilded tricks of monarchs.

The wide range of fertile soil must be trod by Americans
— not Western, nor Eastern, nor Southern men — but
Americans, born, nurtured, and protected by republicanism.
The far-stretching rivers must be covered with the argosies
of American toil, talent, and genius—not of the East, nor
of the South, nor of the West—but of America, of prolific,
fertile, glorious America ! The storms that burst forth with
splendor and stupendous magnificence on this continent
must inspire the souls of Americans—not cow the minds
of men filled with sectional arrogance and dwarfed into
imbecility by sectional conceptions. God's canopy of un-
ceasing beauty must be spread over the proud mien, the
glowing hearts, the pure souls, the profound minds of
American Citizens. The streams must run to refreshen, the
fruits must tempt with luscious nutriment Americans dwelling in the unsullied temple of American republicanism.
Then from behind bright stars brighter spirits will rejoi-
cingly sing over an American Nation, made and perfected—
over a people wise and Christian—" Hail ! Columbia."

Heartiness of sentiment, clearness of object, and steadiness
of purpose, are necessary to make a Nation, Sentiment in-
duces public virtue ; an object is something to realize ; and
a purpose is the volition of public thought that ever works
to realize the object of national existence, permanency and
prosperity. From the days of the Revolution, the sentiment
of the largest portion of the population has been, and is,
freedom for all its inhabitants. The sentiment will have to
be extended and intensified until *the whole* people are influ-
enced by its Christian vibrations. The object of the fathers
of Independence, and of the wise men since seeking sustain-
ing strength at our fathers' graves, was to make the States—
once Colonies—into a strong and compact Republican Na-

tion. The number of the wise has greatly multiplied through and since the "atrocious conspiracy;" but—

"Thanks to fortune, those days of darkness, and anxiety, and doubt, have gone for ever. The dawn has come at last. After that long and fearful night, shaken with tempest and pregnant with terror, watched with throbbing hearts and suspended breath by every loyal American, the sun of freedom has re-arisen, and its glory is streaming over a regenerated land."—*Four Years in Secessia.*

We shall have to agitate and educate until the object is seen and adopted by each man and woman who presses our generous soil. Among them a steady purpose must be invoked,—an ·unfaltering purpose, a never-lessening purpose, to make this land the happy abode of American Republicanism. At work, or in pleasure, or in dreams, the stern resolve, the mighty purpose, must be present to the mind. It must be the ritual of our politics, as the object of Nationality must be the cardinal religion of our politics, and the sentiment must be the Heaven-born prayer of our politics. We must imitate the operations of nature. *They* never cease, never lessen, never tire. We must watch and strive to imitate (as far as He will give us the power) God, who never slackens His mercies nor diminishes His blessings. Ever the stars shine, ever the sun warms, ever the waters refreshen, ever the breezes bring the perfume of flowers to kiss our ready lips ! O men ! O Americans ! for your children's sake—for the sake of the oppressed, groaning in all lands where kings, and emperors, and aristocracies, darken the panting energies of mind—*never cease* to have a mighty purpose, a steadily operating purpose, to make these States the greatest Nation, to save, to succor, to sanctify (through CHRIST) the afflicted of mankind. No spasmodic operations, no furious but only momentary zeal, no mild "campaign"— but a purpose steady, regular, unfaltering as the tides, piercing as the lightning, strong as the seas, grand as nature, beneficent as religion. " A strong pull, a long pull, and a pull altogether," for a perfected American Nationality.

Who will give their money, their time, their energy—in difficulty, in adversity, in storm, till the harvest is reached ? We appeal not so much to the many as to the few who have faith, zeal, and wisdom, for a National party will have to be organized. Not at present, perhaps, but ultimately. Our energy and ability must be devoted to drawing men and women together to give their money and time for the great and necessary work. May these lines prepare the way! A new party will have to combine the elements of National Unity and permanency. A movement in this direction has already commenced among the Germans in New York City. Their *Manifesto* shows that they are animated with the deep importance of the views we are urging. Their efforts are confined among their German brothers. We write to impress the topics most urgently and impressively upon the staid Americans. They are questions of paramount importance to every politician, to every divine, to every merchant and manufacturer, to every publicist. We are sanguine of results, but not hasty—we are fired with zealous faith, but we are not uncalculating. When friends are gathered together, great efforts will be made to thwart their operations, to discourage them, to baffle them, to disband them. Courage ! the laborers for American Nationality will Triumph, just as patriotism and energy Triumphed over a revolting and fiendish rebellion. Through dark and weary nights we may have to watch, through dreary days of lowering clouds—but beyond the nights and the clouds is the golden, cheering, and everlasting sunshine.

One greater than us (though not greater in desire, in zeal, in purity of motive)—one greater than we can ever aspire to be—has spoken words of encouragement very appropriate to the theme that forms the concluding part of this section. We transcribe the words of the Thinker in preference to prolonging our own. We give with pleasure pearls from a wise man's tray, instead of sand from our own poor sack. We present a large tray, but take them all, dear reader, and wear them constantly around your heart and mind. *There* they will shine, and attract the observers whom we require. Let them be seen ! There is no vanity manifested in displaying such costly, such never-fading ornaments. Behold ! for here they are—

" What has been done in the last half-century is a great achievement looked at as history—we may thank God for that—but I had rather look at it as prophecy. The progress in material things in America, the increase in power over nature throughout the Christian world, the rapidity of communication, the desire for freedom of body and soul, the improvements in political institutions and ideas, the progress in churches, and of the laws, and in the great philanthropies of our time—these to me are a prophecy of a noble triumph of mankind, a greater victory of religion than the highest sages ever dared to foretell in their inspired oracles. They all point to a time when man shall be deemed the noblest of God's works, and shall have dominion over nature, and shall develop his spirit to the fulness of the stature of a perfect man. They point to a society where the qualities of a man shall be deemed more and greater than the property of man, or society where the strong shall help the weak ; to a church where respect is paid to human nature, where man reverences the free spiritual individuality of man, where God is worshipped as the Infinite Father, not with fear, but with love ; where religion is supposed to be free piety, free goodness, free thought ; where nature, material and human, is recognized as the scripture of God ; where truth is the creed, and faith and works are the two great forms of communion with God and man ; a church which like this great soul of Christ, goes to seek and save that which is lost, and under him sees Satan falling as lightning out of heaven ; to a state whose statutes recognize the unalienable rights of all men to life, liberty, property, to a free development of their nature ; a state whose law is justice, and the welfare of the negro's child is as carefully cared for as the welfare of the whole state, and any insult offered to it by a man is as promptly redressed as an insult by a nation to the majesty of the state. But, I think history points to a world where the nations shall learn war no more, nor count men of other speech as strangers, but shall seek to make a Christian world where nations shall dwell together, one great family, in love and peace. All this must come. Ideas which are now but sentiments, which are nothing but a tendency will one day be a fact; as Christ's Sermon on the Mount, this will make a new literature, church, state, and world; they will make all things new."

3

" Believing that Political Science has its truths no less than moral, I cannot regard them with indifference, I cannot but wish them to be seen and embraced by others.

" On the other hand, it must not be forgotten that these truths have been much disputed ; that they have not, like moral truths, received that universal assent of good men which makes us shrink from submitting to question. And again, in human affairs, the contest has never been between pure truth and pure error. Neither then may we assume political conclusions as absolutely certain ; nor are political truths ever wholly identical with the professions or practice of any party or individual. If, for the sake of recommending any principle, we disguise the errors or the crimes with which it has been in practice accompanied, and which, in the weakness of human nature, may perhaps be naturally connected with our reception of it, then we are guilty of most blameable partiality. And so it is no less, if for the sake of decrying an erroneous principle, we deprecate the wisdom, and the good and noble feelings with which error also is frequently, and in some instances naturally, joined. This were to make our sense of political truth to overpower our sense of moral truth ; a double error, inasmuch as it is at once the less certain, and by far the less worthy."—T. ARNOLD, D. D.

There are six elements that are the basis of all the combinations that constitute a free, permanent, and progressive nation. The absence of one, or more, of the elements, will produce tyrannical, unjust, or absurd arrangements. Under imperfect combinations from deficient elements, a country can become great, sections of the people prosperous—but not the whole people, not the physical toilers. Of such a country, these words of A. COCHIN are fully applicable :

" Withont doubt, free communities are acquainted with wretchedness ; charity entered into the world together with liberty ; and charity does not suffice for all. But I wish to know whether sick slaves are everywhere treated better than our poor, in Christian hospitals. Is the artisan alone exposed to begging ? May it not also become the lot of the millionaire ? Why does not the author of the argument become himself a slave, through prudence, in order to avoid the risk of dying in a hospital ?"

To no Christian and absolutely " free communities" can COCHIN's words be applied with correctness of facts and judgment. They can be to all old nations and empires—and to our past history and present practice. The mighty changes we have commenced are not completed. The great arch of perfected Republicanism has yet to span our country. A free people, a wise people, a prosperous people, a progressive people, have yet to dwell upon our shores. It may be (it ought to be) the generation of to-day—but if not this, it must be that of to-morrow. Almost (apparently) every law of development of material forces has been studied, largely comprehended, and its science declared. Utopias have been dreamed of by sages and poets, milleniums have been wildly announced by fanatics in the immaturity of unfledged knowledge. New Views, New Lights and " systems," have plagued or aroused communities—but the elements of Republican Nationality, the comprehending of their forces, has not been declared as a science, not even by the best and bravest of our country. " State Rights " doctrine has marred the conceptions and application of National grandeur. Monarchy is the superstition of English politicians, and " State Rights" are the ghoul of our politics. There is a passage in HERBERT SPENCER's *First Principles* that somewhat expresses, on other subjects, what we are insisting upon in relation to the production of American nationality. Our Derbyshire philosopher affirms that—

* * * "The faults of both religion and science have been the faults of imperfect development. Originally a mere rudiment, each has been growing into a more complete form ; the vice of each has in our times been its incompleteness ; the disagreements between them have throughout been nothing more than the consequences of their incompleteness, and as they reach their final forms they come into entire harmony."

To make this passage logically expressive of our views, for " imperfect development," we would say deficient combinations of elements, and that " imperfect development" was the result, and then " incompleteness" would necessarily be the " vice " of deficient combination of elements. Men prate about politics as men palaver about theology, in the folly of ignorance, or in the cant of hypocrisy, or in the narrowness of personal aggrandisement. If there was practised the same charlatanry by professors and students of physical science, we should be still living in the age of " pack-horses," stage-coaches, brimstone matches with flint and steel, blunder-busses, pig-tails, and pretty lasses without life-saving crinoline ! There are fixed laws in politics as in chemistry, physiology, and astronomy—as there are fixed laws governing all combinations and conditions that have a potency in the worlds of matter and of mind. But whoever may be the " guiding star" of politics, the people will have to realize the problem. And where the people are not wise enough to do so, a perishing empire is the frightful finale—a " land of desolation" is the inevitable consequence. In the lapse of ages, the ploughshare is driven by the stranger over the buried foundations of once boastful cities. Alas ! may such *never* be the fate of this people and of this country.

Since the foregoing part of this section was written, we have alighted on a passage by an American author that affirms what we have here somewhat dogmatically indicated. The passage was delivered from various platforms in 1848.

At the risk of being charged with repetition of thought and tautology of expression, we reprint the passage on account of the great importance of the subject (for it cannot be too often mentioned) and the eloquent conciseness of the writer's style. He states that,

" The most marked characteristic of the American nation is a love of freedom, of man's natural rights. This is so plain to a student of American history, or of American politics, that the point requires no arguing. We have a genius for liberty ; the American idea is freedom, natural rights. Accordingly, the work providentially laid out for us to do, seems this,— to organize the rights of man. *This is a problem hitherto unattempted on a national scale in human history.* Often enough attempts have been made to organize the powers of priests, kings, nobles, in a theocracy, monarchy, oligarchy, powers which had no foundation in human duties or human rights, but solely in the selfishness of strong men. Often enough have the *mights* of man been organized, but NOT the RIGHTS OF MAN. Surely there has never been an attempt made, on a national scale, to organize the rights of man, as man ; rights resting on the nature of things ; rights derived from no conventional compact of men with men ; not inherited from past generations, nor received from parliaments and kings, nor secured by their parchments ; but rights that are derived straightway from God, the Author of Duty and the Source of Right, and which are secured in the great charter of our being."

We have taken the liberty to emphasize certain words in the above quotation—words that enunciate the fact and the thought that we are here declaring with all the energy of our pen and the deep emotions of our heart. It is the rights of man in opposition to the wrongs of *color*, of privilege, and of property, that we urge the people to establish—not partially, but completely—not in one State of our Union, but throughout the entire Republic—until its proportions, strength, and beauty, grow into a Nation, never to decay. Over the altar of American freedom let the Cross glow with Heavenly approval, and around it gather the ardent devotees of American Nationality. Let Nationality become part of the practical religion of our lives. Let it animate us with Puritanical firmness, divested of, or rather not to be associated with, narrowness and bigotry. With ports wide open to receive the oppressed, but making the oppressed assimilate themselves with us—to become cells in our large organs, leaving their intellectual as well as their physical rags behind them—we shall be *the only* organizers of the rights of man on the inimitable rock of Christianity. Then we shall have completed and perfected the political work commenced by the temporary English Commonwealth. *Then* the "roll-call" of nations will be read *here,* and answered-to by all the nations. O God ! hasten the day. Let the serpent's head of ignorance, and despotism, and Imperial absolutism, be crushed beneath the car of American Freedom, in which reposes Nationality. Let the Satan of man's crimes against man, and against Thee, O God ! be put to confusion and to flight.

> "Sin-bred, how have ye troubled all mankind
> With shows instead, mere shows of seeming pure,
> And banished from man's life—his happiest life—
> Simplicity and spotless innocence."

The elements of Nationality for American Republicanism are—

(1) UNIVERSAL SUFFRAGE.

(2) UNIFORMITY OF NATURALIZATION.

(3) NATIONAL SYSTEM OF EDUCATION.

(4) UNIFORM SYSTEM OF CURRENCY.

(5) UNIFORM SYSTEM OF POSTAL-INTERCOURSE.

(6) UNFETTERED PRESS AND PULPIT.

Other conditions of nationality are merely evolved from these six elements, as water is evolved from a combination of oxygen and hydrogen gases. For instance, Banking forms *a part* of a system of currency, and national currency really includes Taxation. This will not be admitted by many persons, but close scrutiny will produce the conviction. It is not necessary that we should do much more than enumerate the elements. We do not desire to enter into the merits of rival systems. The unsettled questions among European currency-doctors we do not intend to pronounce upon. The peculiar virtues of paper, and gold, and silver, or any other article, as a medium of Exchange, we are not presumptuous enough to attempt to determine. Our only purpose here is, to insist on the necessity for sound and lasting combinations of the elements of National power, progress, and permanency.

But the *present safety* of our country requires that we recognize and immediately adopt the first and third elements. DELAY *is* DANGEROUS. The qualification for Citizenship must be made National, not left to the whims or tyranny of wealthy or even bigoted poor men in the States. Men *born* on our soil are Americans, be they black or white, and are to be endowed with political power, that is permanent. Where an American lives or travels to (in America) he should have and take with him the rights of American manhood. Those rights should not be lessened nor be abrogated because he leaves one State and emigrates to another. He ought not to be a man in one State and a non-entity in another State. The dignity of a free man should clothe in righteous political power his footsteps and his location. While he is untainted with a desire to injure the life and property of another person, while he does not desire to disorganize his country by violence, he is a man entitled to all the honor and power that society can confer upon him. But if he is more than untainted with crime, if he has *fought* to save the country for other men, as well as for himself, then he is doubly entitled to possess and enjoy political power. If political power is refused to the maimed hero, because God has made him black, or a cross between white and black, then the community so acting is *cursed* with a moral-leper that stinks in the nostrils of good and wise men. A people so acting is doomed to infamy, and will be terror-stricken with the thunders of God's holy mountains. Will this proud American people immolate itself in political darkness? Will it do so while yonder watches the benign Spirit of LINCOLN, over whose bloody corpse but yesterday the people sighed-forth worship, reverence, nay, even adoration for the Apostle of Emancipation, *because* he had Emancipated the oppressed ! In thought, in sentiment, have they not inscribed on the murdered President's tomb—

> " Whose proudest monument shall be,
> The broken fetters of the slave"?

Will Americans become false to worship, recreant to reverence, apostates to adoration ? Will they damn themselves before their tears of anguish can trickle-off their features ! O God ! forbid the sin, the crime, the shame. O God ! let not America be covered with a fresh woe, nor the Heavens be veiled in the blood of more victims, nor the air be filled with the moans of wronged heroes. No ! we will not entertain the horrifying supposition. The soul of LINCOLN will move the great heart of the American people. Political justice, " equal and exact," will sit in an American Republic— crowned with universal approbation.

Not only must education be national, and not left to the caprices of States, but it should be the qualification of *naturalization*. An emigrant who cannot read nor write should not be permitted to become an American Citizen until he can read and write. Nay, a little more, he should be able to give *reasons* for wishing to become an American Republican, in preference to continuing to be the subject of a monarch. If he cannot read nor write, nor give reasons, he is a fool not worth having—whose presence as a Citizen would be a peril to our country. It is not foreign fools, but men, whom we should receive into our household Grown-up children who come *here* must not be termed men, nor treated as the equals of men. If they will come here while they are mere children, they must be sent to and kept at school until they are strong enough to be accepted in the company of men.

We are glad that CHARLES BROOKS (of Medford, Mass.) is devoting his energies to the advocacy of a national system

of education.   Though he seems to have just now to bear
the danger of the battle and the burden of the expense, he
will, in time, see the only fruits he desires to contemplate—
America covered with an educated people ; for education is
the handmaid of freedom—Minerva is the faithful wife of
Liberty.   O blessed pair !   O happy dispensers of earthly
joys !   And he who has long striven to bring you together
into "the holy bonds of matrimony" is one CHARLES BROOKS,
of worthy reputation.

   It will be unfair to our readers, "too bad" to those who
give us their patience, if we pass from the subject of education without informing them that the works of C. BROOKS
are published in a reasonable form, and can be procured at
863 Broadway, New York City.   Those who would like to
go over the whole question of national education, should peruse the earnest essays of the Medford publicist.

" The long sacrifice completed and accepted. Indivisible Nationality and universal liberty bought and paid for—paid for with a heavy price— but *paid for*. In the Past, the toil and sacrifice, the doubt and fear, the blood and anguish, and in the Past, the sin. In the Future, peace, and Union, and prosperity, and glory unspeakable."—*Professor* Searing's *Lincoln in History*.

And now, farewell !

> " A word that must be, and hath been,
> A sound which makes us linger."

If we place many more pages before you, patient reader, you will become wearied with our excess of zeal, earnestness, and repetition of opinions. Yet the subjects are so important, involving the welfare of American Republicanism and the progress of humanity, that we must still " linger." Though chilling winds blow strongly—though the dews fall thickly— though birds hie away swiftly to retreats in green and shady spots—though violets droop in the balmy regions of repose— who can resist the charming temptation to remain gazing on the golden glories of the sun, as they fade into the purple realms of Night's bright queen ? A mother's voice may call to chide for careless exposure to unseen dangers, but for once that call of devoted affection is unheeded. Day seems to be giving its parting smile of satisfaction—its benison of Good-Morrow ! to all the earth—and we still linger to watch and admire, though in so doing we are disobedient to her who brought us forth in agony as well as in gladness ! When

TUBAL CAIN lays down his hammer and himself, when the mill-stream ceases to sing its song of gleesome industry, when the plough reclines to rest itself against "the old oak tree," when troops of fairies arrange to sleep in the pellucid cells of aromatic flowers, and put on for night-robes the gorgeous colors—when Neptune watches the good ship as she moves along in starry rays, while hardy mariners are resting from toils that are sweetened with honest purposes—we muse in happy thought upon the blissful scene. And as we look on America's achievements, her joys yearly outnumbering her woes, her sublime victories in the midst of great perils, her face gradually brightened with happiness, her strength merging into beauty, her strifes into blessings, her noisy words into heroic actions, the dreams of her poets more than realized in the acts of her Congress of patriots, her Prosperity beckoning the world's Pauperism to revivifying "homesteads"— who can look on such wonders without lingering, tenderly lingering, and resolving to labor in completing and perfecting the work that has been so nobly commenced ? *Here* the dreams of the entranced poets of all times and climes are destined to be realized, *here* the blood of the martyrs of all lands will be transformed into fragrant flowers, *here* the toils of patient and enduring scholars will be rewarded by the banishment of ignorance from humanity, *here* all the righteousness of God's Word shall be produced when American Republicanism is fashioned into *a* National American Republic.

My brother, clasp hands with me—my sister, stand with us, and twine the garlands of freedom, of knowledge, of wisdom, of progress, of Christian sanctity around us—but so twine them that, as each brother and sister comes, *they* can be taken within the zone of happiness.

FAREWELL !

APPENDICES.

————•◆•————

A TOPIC FOR AMERICA'S STATESMEN.

Amid the clash of arms, questions of profound importance are not likely to be contemplated by the mass of the people. Strong eyes are required to look through the smoke, and gaze upon our nation's future. But the rebellion is near its unalterable doom, and we may pause to consider another grave topic.

The tide of emigration rolls bravely to our shores. When the rebellion is crushed, emigration will rush with feverish desire and hope to this country. We do not object to the emigrant-tide—we hail it with hearty greeting. But the rubbish it washes from old countries to our cities we dislike. Seething ignorance, fanatical prejudices, united to the bigotry of creeds, spread a moral pestilence in our prominent cities, and darken the glory of our nation's grandeur. The majesty of this republic is imperilled by foreign ignorance and destitution. We have not only to *feed* the pauper multitudes of monarchies, but we have to educate them, or be poisoned by their presence. We turn not from the task of feeding the honest, nor of instructing the willing ; but we dislike to be pestered with the lazy, the brutishly ignorant, and the helplessly destitute, created by Europe, and flung upon our shores. These mobs have been a trouble to us, and they will be a trouble to us again if we are not wise in time.

The ragged mobs *will* come ; the wretched hordes of ignorance will come ; the vile herds of aristocratic misrule will come here for safety and for succor. We cannot prevent them. Our statesmen must accept the fact, and *use* it for our country's permanent welfare. What will have to be done is this—*not allow monarchical mud to accumulate in our most important cities.*

What we have to dread is the concentrating of ignorance, national antipathies, and unpenetrated bigotry. The power of political parties, based on foreign ignorance, must no longer be tolerated nor permitted. The emigrant-tide must be directed to run into the arterial system of our country's health. Every foreigner must be lost in his assimilation with our healthy nation. Excrescences should be removed by adoption into the blood of republican health. The task is an ungracious one, but our nation's safety requires its accomplishment. The work of manuring land is not pleasant, but necessary. And statesmen are political agriculturists, manuring and planting in season, so that the harvest of national greatness and stability may be reaped for the whole future.

We write more to attract earnest attention than to propose plans. We have our own way of removing the evil, but it requires money, industry, and iron firmness. The importance of the subject is vast, and requires much thought and more energy. The subject cannot be warded off; it must be grappled with. Emigrants we require, but not bad ones. If people come here to thrive, they should come educated for thriving. If they will not come here prepared, they have no right to complain if we treat them sternly, and insist that *they* comply with our plans for their improvement and our safety. "Ferocious philanthropists," who insult the characteristics of nations, have not our sympathy. Men who excite the passions of races are not the wise friends of this republic. We would purge vices from us by an appeal to the virtues of races and creeds. We will not denounce names and good intentions; but we will strive to destroy the sins that would, otherwise, destroy this home of freedom. We will not consent to feed famishing multitudes from Europe, at the sacrifice of our permanent progress on the highway of civilization.

W. W. B.

From *The New York Citizen*, April 1st, 1865.

FACE THE DANGER.

It is cowardly to shrink from danger ; it is unpatriotic to murmur at the necessity even of a constant outlay of time, money, and energy. Great wisdom and devotion are necessary for the reforming of great abuses and the suppression of great evils. Success is a chaplet given only to patient labor. First, cheerless toil—then the seed is sown and watched anxiously in storm and sunshine—finally the harvest is reaped—the corn is garnered under the inspiring influence of the pipe and the tabor !

Old evils cannot be easily removed, but cleared away they *can be* by those who combine in themselves the patriot and the philosopher, and the Christian moralist.

To face a danger manfully is to comprehend its nature and its power. Our weakness in extending and deepening the power of goodness is in proportion to our ignorance of the precise nature and mode of evil. We must see an antagonist before we can measure him. We imitate the wondrous charms and glowing beauties of nature after we have seen them. The skilful general advances when from his scouts he learns the position and number of his enemy's forces, and wins when he knows his enemy's weakness. The shout of victory is for the strong, because knowledge and wisdom give irresistible strength. Knowledge, prudence, patience, and perseverance, are the laws governing the elements and controlling their combinations. Our country is now mighty, but a divine magnificence is before us, and we can reach it if we are wise and perpetually heroic in our conduct.

The concentrating of ignorant multitudes in cities is dangerous to the morals and stability of a State. People can be moral and unlearned, but they cannot be ignorant and moral. There must be knowledge of some kind and amount to produce consciousness, and consciousness is the basis of morals. Every extension of knowledge enlarges the republic of morals. Clever men are sometimes dissolute, learned men are

sometimes depraved ; but as compared with the totality of
society, they are exceptional. A knowledge of the laws of
light, heat, and air, shows us the necessity of improving the
structure of our homes ; improved homes sustain and prolong our health ; health gives the power to think, and
thought generates wisdom and goodness, to be sanctified by
religion. Ignorance, however, is the producer of disease,
imbecility, and reckless depravity. It concentrates in sweat-
ing masses of human filth. It vegetates in "slums," it lux-
uriates in "alleys," in "closes," and "wynds," and in
fever-creating "tenements" of our rich city. It revels in
darkness and fatalism. It screeches around the stoves of
"night-houses" in rags, obscenity, and stinks. It brays
with savage joy, stimulated by rum and the "sweets of
office," under the influence of the cunning and hypocrisy of
party factions and wretched public tricksters. It is at the
call of every political knave, and gleesomely follows in the
trail of its own destruction. It is a pest and a nuisance—
appalling the timid and disgusting the wise. Such ignorance
we have festering in this city. It poisons our air, it stifles
our morals, it impedes our progress. It blights the infant's
growth, it makes a pestilence in our streets, and converts
political gatherings into hells of knavish passions. It adores
false gods, worships mere animality, and reverences political
scoundrelism. This is the kind of ignorance the pauperized
mobs of Europe bring to our shores. Here it comes for succor and for safety, and when both are obtained, it turns upon
its adopted mother to rend her for her kindness ! O ingrati-
tude ! thy name is—Emigrants.

When war's dead blast has ceased, when treason against
national freedom and prosperity has ceased, *then* the peril of
our country will be the ignorance of emigrants festering in
our cities. It is a difficulty that puzzles many, for its foul
breath penetrates the whole atmosphere of our country's
welfare. Cannon-balls cannot scatter the evil, for it is intellectual and social in its influences, and cannot be treated
with physical remedies. Yet the disease must be carefully
examined, carefully watched, and wisely doctored. The

emigrant patient is dangerously ill ; *our* health is jeopardized by the continuance of the disease. Help ! or we perish. This is an evil that all wise and good people should help to remove. The danger to ourselves daily increases. Every hour brings a fresh blast of moral pestilence to our shores. In a few more weeks the nuisance will be trebled. Prepare yourselves to FACE THE DANGER.

W. W. B.

NEW YORK, *June*, 1865.

THE SITUATION.

Tired, after four years of energetic war, the people (as a people) are not only in a state of torpor, but are rapidly becoming politically too oblivious. Rebels are pardoned hourly who have *not* repented, nor changed their desires. The old monarchical oppression of regulating wages is being done in Georgia, and the *lowest* rate is being awarded to the emancipated. Schools for little ones are closed through the brutality inflicted on the helpless by the Southern " chivalry." The disintegrating doctrine of complete State Rights is being preached in high places before rebels, and *for* rebels, who lately murdered our soldiers and tried to crucify our republic. " Let *each* state judge of *the depository* of its own political power." A pretty doctrine to preach to unrepentant sinners ! A comforting creed to be adopted in rebel States ! Verily the nation is drunk with victory, and blinded with a splendid military success.

Street brawls, intimidation of Union men—because the people are asleep, instead of being wide-awake to practise justice and generosity. Aye ! generosity to the black men who fought for us, bled for us, and may have died for us. Heroism is not to be rewarded because it throbs for freedom and nationality within an ebony casket. Oh ! foul injustice, and withering wrong !

In every rebel State, loyal men will be outvoted, derided, and subjected to intimidation. Who can prevent such pro-

4

ceedings ? Either there must be military occupation and
military government for at least the next twelve months, or
the black man must have the suffrage. The common sense
view of the position of affairs is unheeded. The military
forces are being withdrawn, the emancipated are not protected, and oath-breaking rebels are voting !

Earnest men are beings scared from giving the negro the vote
by the bug-a-boo, ignorance. It is the old trick of tyrants.
The same thing is being attempted in England just now.
There the fears of the middle-classes are being acted on, so
that they will shrink from introducing the operatives to political power. Those who think the colored people down
South are more ignorant than the whites in rebel States, let
them carefully read the guarded statements and cheering
facts given by the Rev. Charles Lowe in his " Discourse on
the Condition and Prospects of the South." The truth is
that the blacks are more intellectually *inclined* than the
whites—and the demonstration is that *they are* realizing, in
proportion to their means, the praiseworthy inclination. But
suppose they did not, what then ? Ignorance is merely a
relative term. We are all ignorant to each other, and we
are all wise to each other. The density of our ignorance and
the extent of our wisdom depend on training, natural volition,
experience, surroundings, and opportunities. Some blacks
are idiotic, and so are many whites. Many whites are great
mathematicians, and so are some blacks ! God alone, and
not presumptuous men, should strike down with thunderbolts
a man's rights and a man's manliness.

And we are to discuss this suffrage question persistently
and earnestly in the temple of American Republicanism ! The
Declaration of Independence is not yet understood, because
the people are too inclined to accept the plausible dogmas of
interested leaders.

So be it. We *will* discuss the question ; the discussion
shall be *the* question throughout the land. We will discuss
the topic till sinners are abashed, traitors disconcerted, and
hypocrites are made powerless. We will discuss the subject
until the wronged are righted, the down-trodden are uplifted,

and God's laws are fulfilled—until the people are no longer
" blind, as though without sight."

W. W. B.

From *The Commonwealth*, July 8th, 1865.

INDEPENDENCE EVE IN A NEW YORK VILLAGE.

NEW YORK, July 10, 1865.

Slowly recovering from what appeared to be a bed of death,
not strong enough to endure the noise of Bowery, nor the
rushing, pushing, tearing, and roaring of Broadway, I resolved
to pass the fourth of July in the perfumed air of Morrisania.
Arriving there on the eve of Independence, I was invited to
the Congregational Church to participate in a "jubilee." I
went and had a treat. A respectable audience, of nearly
three hundred ladies and gentleman, was present.

The pastor of the church (Rev. Mr. Gladden) presided.
His face shone with enthusiasm, and his voice was musical as
evening bells. F. W. Tappan read the Declaration of Independence, and, after he did so, gave a brief history of the Revolution. His speech was discriminating and well arranged.
Col. O. T. Beard followed. The choir then sent forth its
grand notes, that thrilled all hearts with a renewed devotion
to freedom and justice. When the soft charm for a moment
ceased, the Hon. W. T. B. Milliken rose to pour forth warn-
ing and encouragement in pellucid streams of unaffected eloquence. He told of the day when his children were insulted
for belonging to an Abolitionist !—of the time when only one
pastor in the village dared to demand liberty for God's children clothed in sable. And the speaker in fiery words insisted that the negroes must have the same freedom and justice
as white men enjoy in this country. It was a treat to listen
to this old and earnest anti-slavery man, to this zealous friend
of Christian progress for *all* men, irrespective of creed and
color. As the Rev. S. Bourne rose to conclude the night's
speaking, it seemed that a divine sanction and blessing were
being given to Mr. Milliken for his powerful and noble words.

"Amen!" was the first word uttered by the reverend speaker. "And it seems," he said, "as though I could only repeat amen! to Mr. Milliken's words of truth, freedom, and justice." And, reverend brother, we re-echo your most Godly "Amen!"

The singing of the choir was excellent. "Roll on, thou ship of state," "The Victory is Ours," and the following hymn, were sung with feeling, taste, and delicacy of execution. This hymn was given immediately after the Declaration of Independence had been read :—

"O glorious Words! we hail at last
   Your pledge of Liberty!
It mocked our hope through all the past,
   But now, the land is FREE!

"O glorious Day! thy dawn shall sweep
   The land from sea to sea;
But touch no spot where bondmen weep,
   For all the land is free!

"O glorious Banner! forth we fling
   Thy folds triumphantly!
And 'neath thy blood-washed brightness sing,
   'To-day the land is free!'

"Our trembling faith is changed to sight
   Of better days to be,
When Love shall rule and Peace shall right
   The land whose soil is free!

"O God! we grasp Thy guiding hand;
   The praise belongs to Thee!
And, trusting Thee, our happy land
   Shall be forever FREE!"

We returned to our old friends' home in Morrisania, and went to sleep and dreamed of broken fetters, a king denied, rebels conquered, and happy smiles gleaming across the once sad faces of the emancipated. O blessed dream! O happy night! for in our visions we saw rewards given in Heaven to the angels who had worked on earth for the destitute and oppressed.   W. W. B.

SUFFRAGE MEETING AT NEWARK, N. J.

NEWARK, N. J., *July* 11, 1865.

A very influential audience of ladies and gentlemen was present last (Monday) evening, in the "Library Hall," in this city. It had been announced in the press that Mr. W. W. Broom, of the New York Loyal Publication Society, would deliver an address on "Reconstruction." At the time appointed, B. S. Morehouse was voted to the chair, and introduced the speaker in flattering terms.

Mr. Broom commenced by saying, "If there are any persons present who have corns they do not desire to be trod on, prejudices they object to have probed, bigotry they desire to hug, they had better retire at once ; but if you wish for truth, for earnest and unsparing investigation, I shall be pleased to have you remain till I resume my seat." Not one left, but many more swelled the audience.

Mr. Broom then proceeded to descant on the past and present condition of the South, of the present incompleteness of our military triumph, of the cruel treatment awarded to the emancipated. During his long address, he frequently referred to the Declaration of Independence and the preamble to the Constitution. He answered the objections that are mooted against the suffrage, proved their absurdity, and manifested their injustice. He insisted that the nation should realize in its practice the doctrines it had fought for upon every field ; that pure republicanism should live and progress on this continent, not crumble away like the empires of old.

The speaker was often applauded, and when he sat down, he was greeted with a perfect ovation of cheers, that was continued for several minutes. When the applause subsided, Mr. Broom again rose and said, "Ladies and gentlemen, I desire to have your vote on the opinions I have advanced. I want to ascertain how many of you are for complete justice for *all* men and women, *irrespective* of color." The Chairman proceeded to put the question to the vote, and there was a unanimous and hearty response given for suffrage for black as well as white men.

After a vote of thanks was awarded to the speaker, the meeting was adjourned. Old and young crowded around the stand and invited Mr. Broom to revisit Newark, and to assist in the fall campaign in Jersey state. Mr. Broom cheerfully consented to do so, as far as his feeble health would permit.

From *The Commonwealth.*

A LECTURE ON RECONSTRUCTION.

NEW YORK, *July* 24, 1865.

An influential society of ladies and gentlemen in New York city, requested Mr. W. W. Broom (of whom you have before spoken) to give his views on Reconstruction. He did so on Tuesday evening, July 18th, in the lodge-room, 835 Broadway. The chair was taken by J. H. Edgerley, and the proceedings were opened with prayer by the Rev. Mr. Stuart. After prayer, Mrs. L. M. Bronson (the gifted wife of Prof. Bronson) read the following poem in her peculiarly charming style :—

THE WAR CRY—"NO MASTER, OR SLAVE."

BY MRS. L. M. BRONSON.

O! do you remember how bright the stars shone,
And girdled the Heavens, with glittering zone,
When (on electric wing) strange words came flying ?
" To arms ! ye Freemen ! The war-cry is ringing !
Awake ! sons of Freedom ! Arise in your might !"
Up ! Be ready *all*, to battle for the Right !
Lo, Treason hath stole in, with poisonous breath !
And Sumter's brave sons are now grappling with death !"
O! God ! how our hearts throbbed and our brains ran wild
To see our old flag by rank traitors defiled !
It stirred the true blood to make it ever wave ;
To call no man master, and no man—a slave !

Borne on winged winds over mountain and glen,
Flashed the thrilling words, firing the hearts of men !
And grandly back again with majestic form,
(Like the sullen wrath of the dark gathering storm,)
Come with thundering and mighty tread sublime,
Ten hundred thousand men forming into line !

With calm and steady eye, with firm and loyal mien,
Around their Chief they stand ; "The flag shall wave again !"
They swear the immortal oath as Freemen only can,
To plant it on the grave of each traitor man ;
For roused is true blood, to make it ever wave,
To call no man master, and no man a slave!

List! the battle's rage! Lo, contest—hand to hand,
Bursting shells light the sea and desolate the land!
Never before, through the long line of Ages,
Hath such treach'rous war darkened history's pages ;
Flowing crystal stream, mountain, hill and plain,
Are crimsoned with the blood of our nobles slain ;
Earth drinks the loyal gore, and thirsts even yet.
She loves the precious rain, falling " warm and wet ;"
For it tasteth sweet, as in days by-gone ;
As it did on Bunker's Hill, and at Lexington.
For roused is the true blood to make the old flag wave
To call no man master, and no man a slave!

Words giving Freedom, most nobly were spoken,
They thrilled the whole land, as a Heaven-sent token,
White-winged angels heard the echoes afar
And came thronging in hosts to speed on the war ;
A march triumphant is heard throughout the land,
For the Lord God of Hosts hath stretched forth his hand !
Our fathers won victory ; we'll crown her again,
Though gory the wreath, with our thousands of slain.
Now, proudly, we hail our old banner, so bright ;
Whose broad folds are floating for Justice and Right.
And strong are our hearts, while the old flag shall wave
To call no man master, and no man a slave !

'Tis worth the great battles, 'tis worth all our pain,
To measure the strength of our nation again ;
We knew not its greatness, nor dreamed of its power ;
We felt not how sweet and how priceless the dower,
Bequeathed by great souls, who have passed on to God,
Till smote by the Lord with his chastening rod.
Then, great spirits arose with purposes high—
With the daring of soul, to conquer, or die.
Can we ever forget how nobly and brave
They have fought on the land and fought on the wave ?
How fixed were their souls to make the old flag wave
To call no man master, and no man a slave ?

After the poem was read, Mr. Broom was introduced to the assembly amid hearty cheering. During more than an hour, he dilated on the past and present condition of society in the Southern and Northern States. He insisted that "equal and exact justice to all men" must be the principle, the rule, and the law of this great modern republic. He urged that as a matter of permanent safety, of justice, of reward for perils endured, loyal blacks should have the suffrage given to them. On the ground of economy, of morality, of republicanism, of religion, he said, we are bound to make this continent a veritable New World for those who have been pauperized and oppressed. He described how suddenly the nation had become a magnificent naval and military power, and now the people must become equally strong and powerful in wisdom, justice, and progress. He gave many facts about the emancipated with Saxon energy, and clothed them in the graces of poetic language. Mr. Broom was frequently interrupted with bursts of applause, and when he resumed his seat, thanks were presented to him with great enthusiasm.

From *The Commonwealth.*

SOUTH CAROLINA'S LAWS.

Act of 1820 declares, that no slave should hereafter be emancipated but by an act of the Legislature.

By the Act of 1834, slaves are prohibited to be taught to read or write, under a penalty, if a white person offend, not exceeding one hundred dollars fine and six months' imprisonment; if a free person of *color* offend, not exceeding fifty lashes and a fine of fifty dollars. The same Act prohibits the employment of a slave or *free person of color* as a clerk or salesman, under a penalty not exceeding one hundred dollars fine, and imprisonment for six months.

In 1848, the Legislature declared, that any bequest, deed of trust, or conveyance, intended to take effect after the death of the owner, whereby the removal of any slave without the State is secured, or intended, with a view to the *emancipation* of such slave, *shall be void.* And that every device or bequest to a slave or slaves, or to any person upon a trust or confidence, secret or expressed, for the benefit of any slave or slaves, shall be void.

Act of 1740, the owners of slaves to provide them with sufficient clothing, covering, and food, and if they should fail to do so, the magistrate is authorized to hear and determine the complaint, and make such order as will give relief, and may set a fine, not exceeding thirty dollars and sixty cents on the owner. HON. T. B. O'NEAL, a Judge, states, " I regret to say that there is, in such a State as ours, great occasion for the enforcement of such a law."

" No master was to allow his slaves to have their own time, nor to plant for themselves any corn, peas, or rice, or to keep any stock of hogs, cattle, or horses."

" Death was the punishment of any person who, by promising freedom in another country, induced a slave to leave the province, and the punishment, also, of the slave if taken. Any slave running away for twenty days was, for the first offence, publicly and *severely* whipped; for the second offence, the runaway was to be branded with the letter R, on the right cheek ; if the master omitted to do this, *he* was fined £10."— M. HOWITT'S *Hist. of America.*

ITEMS WORTH REMEMBERING.

" In South Carolina, Virginia, and Louisiana, life may be taken according to law, *without* intervention of grand or petit jury." " In Louisiana, if the Court is equally divided as to the guilt of a slave, judgment is recorded *against* him."

" A *free* negro coming into the State (of Maryland) is liable to a fine of fifty dollars for every week he remains in it. If he cannot pay the fine, *he is sold.*"

UNIVERSAL SUFFRAGE.

UNIVERSAL SUFFRAGE IN THE REBEL STATES—JUSTICE TO THE NEGRO—AND SAFETY TO THE REPUBLIC !

A MANIFESTO OF THE GERMAN "UNIONBUND" OF NEW YORK.

[Translated from the German for *The Commonwealth.*]

The Reconstruction of the Union is the great problem of the present. On its solution depends whether the blessings of peace shall compensate the nation for all the sacrifices made, or whether discord, or perhaps, even bloody struggles, shall rage between the democratic republicanism of the North and the aristocracy of the South.

State-sovereignty and *slavery* have been the enemies of the Union. Our heroic armies have struck them down. Shall now a blind policy uplift the prostrate foes and enable them to again assail the republic ? Will the nation, better informed than the fathers of the Constitution, allow that the germ of the old evil be preserved in the reconstructed Union? Shall the essence of state sovereignty and of slavery, in the disguise of State Rights and *disfranchisement of the colored people*, be the basis of the new structure of the Union ? That will be the case, if the people do not immediately and with firmness declare and enforce their will.

The " Unionbund " therefore deems it a duty to submit to the German-Americans its views and demands concerning the Reconstruction.

The foundation of the Union was the work of a Convention elected by all the free people, and—South Carolina and Georgia excepted—without distinction as to race. Now, scarcely has the enemy laid down his arms when the reconstruction of the Union is undertaken by the executive alone, and with a haste that does not admit a careful examination and consideration of the state of things.

Congress is not called to co-operate in this important work, nor is time given to the nation to express its will. The Executive assailed (one might say *conquered*) by swarms of delegates from the Southern States, so suddenly converted to loyalty, is about to reconstruct the Union with the materials of the rebellion.

Let the cunning aristocrats of the South be jubilant, let their Northern friends praise the wisdom of the President, let politicians try to evade this burning question,—the independent Citizens tell the whole truth of their conviction to the public servant whom they have elected.

There is no space here for the examination of the question, —"Has the Executive the right to establish the system of reconstructing the rebellious States according to his own views and without the concurrence of Congress?" But it is evident, that in assuming such a power, the Executive acts contrary to the spirit of our institutions. The necessities of the war claimed from the nation many concessions to the Executive ; now that peace is restored, the people have the more firmly to oppose any extension of its sphere.

The convening of Congress for co-operation in the work of Reconstruction seems to us to be a duty of the President, and undoubtedly it would have been an act of wise statesmanship. If slighted, Congress will act with a feeling of wounded pride and violated privilege. To the inevitable conflict of views there will be added the bitter conflict of passions. The immediate co-operation of Congress and the Executive might have led to harmony of views and unity of action, whilst the self-willed proceedings of the President have already had fatal consequences. The leaders of the patriotic party have pronounced against the President's plan of Reconstruction ; the Union phalanx is threatened with disruption, and the enemies of the good cause prepare themselves to rush triumphantly through this breach.

Pregnant with disasters in the determination of the President of granting already now to the rebel States the right to reconstitute themselves. They will have the power to decide questions involving the welfare of the Union according to their interested views, and independently of the national government. The result of the immediate reorganization of the South, by the South itself, will certainly be of such a nature that neither the nation nor Congress can accept it. But what a series of difficulties and struggles will be the consequence of such a conflict !

Of so many ominous questions which may arise from a conflict between the Congress and the Executive, let us mention but one :—" What will be the state of the republic, if Congress persists in refusing admittance to the representatives chosen by the reorganized States, whilst the President sustains them as legally elected, and refuses to alter the state of things in the South ?"

Not a hasty reörganization, but a thorough preparation for a salutary Reconstruction of the Union, is what is needed now for the conquered rebel States. A wise and energetic guardianship, to which the National government is entitled by the laws of war, is for a time the only *régime* applicable to the South. The strong hand of the National power alone can mould the rebel States into faithful members of the Union, and harmonize them with the free people of the North. Without the military protection of the federal government, the truly loyal Citizens of the South will have no influence in the Reconstruction of their States ; nay more—under the system of Reconstruction, initiated by the President, they will not have any more security of life than they had under the sway of Jefferson Davis. This has been said to the President by Southern men whose loyalty has passed through the ordeal of persecution and exile.

If the Southern States are reconstructed on the President's plan, the colored population, to whose protection and liberation the nation is in honor bound, will fall back under the exclusive rule of its enemies. But too many sad facts show already what then will be for the colored people the value of emancipation and the promise of equal rights ! Has not reorganized Tennessee made of her colored people real serfs ? Has not Holden, the Reconstruction governor of North Carolina, declared, " The white race is the ruling race, and has the right to remove the colored people from the State" ? What is to be expected from Sharkey, the governor of Mississippi,—from that man, who, as a judge, committed the infamy of sending back to slavery a colored woman with her child, the offspring of a repentant planter, who, by his last will, had given them their liberty ?

Even now, under the flag of the Union, the aristocrats of the South begin to exercise their old tyranny, because they see in the policy of the President the return of their power, restored by the immediate exercise of State Rights. For that reason, the rebels, following the advice of Reverdy Johnson, hasten to take the oath of allegiance. These metamorphosed rebels calculate already with their friends at the North the time when they will again have the majority in Congress, and the power in the White House,—even more, they dare openly propose a bargain, involving political treason, to the successor of the Martyr of the Union and of emancipation.

The President's policy of Reconstruction is the beginning of reaction ; its consequences will be fatal, though he be animated with the best intentions, and is, as many of his defenders say, making now only an experiment of one system, and is ready to be corrected by the course of events.

The President and the true friends of the republic will perhaps in future struggle in vain against the accomplished facts. What the nation wants is not a double-faced trial, but a clear, firm system, answering to the feelings and the convictions to which the free people of the North have been elevated by the great events of the last four years. In the loyal States, the liberal Citizens are already laboring to lay the foundation of equal rights for the Reconstruction of the Union. It is the duty of the federal government to do the same in the South before the conquered rebel States can exercise again their rights as members of the Union.

The rebellion of the South, made by the States as States, and by all their constituted authorities, has, as far as the Union is concerned, abrogated all previously-existing Constitutions and Laws of those States. In reconstructing the Union, the national government has therefore to deal only with their populations. To give them a Republican government is the right and the duty of the federal power. But this right embraces *everything* or *nothing*.

If the President thinks that he has the right to appoint
governors to the conquered rebel States, he has also the right
to call on their whole loyal population for the establishment
of a republican government.   Still more ; a truly republican
government can only be established by the *whole* loyal population, and not by classes arbitrarily selected.   The Proclamation of Emancipation has made free citizens, endowed with
equal rights, of all the inhabitants of the South.   The President cannot be permitted again to erect, with the help of
the abolished slave laws, the barriers formerly existing between the white and colored population.   It is the duty of
the President to defend as faithfully the rights of the colored
people as those of the poor whites of the South, of whom
he considers himself the special representative.   And never
more than in the present emergency will full justice also be
sound statesmanship.   The exclusion of the colored population of the South from the work of Reconstruction would be
a source of infinite evil, as has been the toleration of slavery·
by the Constitution.

Under the guardianship of the federal government, exercised over the conquered States, the emancipated people of
the South have to be transformed into Citizens, made free and
independent by labor and property, and capable of exercising
their civic rights, in order that they may co-operate with
their loyal white fellow-citizens in the great work of reconstructing the Union, when the time shall come.

But the President has declared that there is no necessity
of Reconstruction, that the Southern States possess to-day all
the rights—that of slavery excepted—which they had before
the rebellion.   Is this not surrendering the victory of the
National sovereignty, obtained by the sacrifice of the lives of
so many patriots ?   Is it not necessary that the supremacy
of the national sovereignty should be recognized and *felt*
for a certain time, by the South, in order that they may
learn that State Sovereignty is really dead ?   Will not the
truculent and obstinate aristocracy of the South find, in the
declaration of the President, a reason for considering these
State Rights essentially the same thing—what they called

State Sovereignty before their defeat ?   Should any one be
credulous or simple-minded enough to feel assured, by the
hypocritical promises now made by the Southern crowd
streaming into the White House, let him remember what
has been said of the Bourbons—" They learned nothing, and
forgot nothing !"

To destroy forever the spirit of rebellion it is necessary
that the words of the President should become a fact,—
" *Crime must meet with its punishment !*"   It is, therefore,
to be regretted that, before even one single act of justice has
branded treason and rebellion, the pardoning power of the
President should be exercised with a daily-increasing rapidity, and in so many cases bestowing its benefits on persons
guilty of infamous crimes.   Is it surprising that the people
begin to doubt the realization of the declaration made by the
President ?

These numerous pardons, the Constitutionality of which is
doubted by many, will soon have exhausted the list of ex-
ceptions made by the President himself.   The Union will
lose thereby the legal means of destroying forever the real
power of the criminal aristocracy of the South.   Those
enemies of the Union and of a truly democratic society must
be sentenced as guilty of high treason ; their property must
be seized in order to pay the expenses of the war which they
have originated.   Thus only can the victory of the Northern
society of free labor over the landed monopoly of the Southern aristocracy be secured, and become a source of blessings
to the republic.

The emancipation and the granting of equal political
rights to the colored people are not sufficient to accomplish
the work of Reconstruction.   The landless inhabitants of the
South—the whites as well as the blacks—must obtain possession, by purchase or donation, of the confiscated estates of
the aristocracy, in order that they become really independent
Citizens of the regenerated Republic.

The treasonable undertakings of the Southern aristocracy
have inaugurated not only a political, but also a social revolution.   The victorious arms of the Union have given the

Federal Government the right to close this revolution in a manner which insures the welfare of the Republic. But if this is not done now, the bloody war for the preservation of the National Unity may be followed by the more terrible and dangerous war of the oppressed against their oppressors, which in this case will be the war of one race against the other.

The people must, therefore, as in ancient Rome, tell the government—"Take care that the Republic be not endangered!" The "Unionbund" appeals to all liberal German-Americans to join its ranks, in order to labor together with the American-born Citizens of the same conviction for the realization of the principles of our great revolution.

The "Unionbund" remains faithful to the banner of freedom and justice, borne in the new campaign by the patriots, Sherman, Sumner, Ashley, Chase, Winter Davis, Butler, Pomeroy, Wilson, and others.

On behalf of the "Unionbund," the General Committee.

DR. FREDERICK SCHUETZ, *President.*

DR. H. GULECKE, *Recording Secretary.*

NEW YORK, *July* 15, 1865.

WM. T. BLODGETT, ESQ.

EDITOR OF COMMONWEALTH : The genial patriotism and solid worth of this eminent New York merchant should be known to our Massachusetts citizens. He was the originator (or mainly so) of the New York Loyal Publication Society, and has been, and still is, its laborious Chairman of the Executive Committee. As President of the New York Athenæum Club, his influence is considerable and widely felt. His urbanity and exuberant generosity have been connected with every organization that our late struggle called into existence, in the Empire State. He is now on a lengthened tour in Europe to form a personal friendship with the eminent friends of our country. A few weeks since he was entertained at a dinner with John Bright, and other active English Liberals. In one of his interesting letters, Mr. Blodgett says :

"Since my arrival in London, I have had much to interest and amuse me. One of the most agreeable and ardent friends of our country I have found in John Bright! He is thoroughly and intensely American, and grasps the real beauty of opinion in America with more clearness than any man I have met here, be he American or English.

"I hear but one thought and one feeling expressed since the capture of Jeff. Davis. The first thing that is said, is :—'What are you going to do with Mr. Davis? I hope you are not going to hang him?' &c., &c. Not one thought of the great principles at stake in our country for the progress of freedom and civilization! I don't pretend to argue with such people, for there is no possibility of driving a principle into people's heads who do not wish to be convinced of what we are doing in America. One thing is dawning on the English mind, and that is shown everywhere among intelligent minds here, and that is, that America is a *great* power, and recognized as such among the nations of the earth. You will find that we shall make a sensation when we sneeze, mark my words! They cannot understand us, and wonder to see the first steps being taken toward Reconstruction, and 'stocks' advancing daily—and the people of England notice every minute detail."

We hope to see published the important particulars of travel by so shrewd an observer, whose sources of information are so numerous.

W. T. Blodgett is an able and pleasing speaker, though it is not often he can be induced to speak from New York stands. He prefers to do "good by stealth," and blushes when 'tis named. His speech in London, at the Fourth of July banquet, struck melody, the melody of grateful affection, from every American who was present. What a sweet theme he had to discourse about! It was the women, it was the gentle, loving, patriotic women of America! He told of the daring and precious deeds done by the daughters of freedom, by the dear children of Republican progress. We reprint his speech for the sake of the beautiful subject of his manly eloquence.

THE CHARACTER OF AMERICA'S LADIES.

He could not see the reason why, in a convivial meeting like the present, the toast of "The ladies" should be last, when in men's thoughts they

were always first. At that late hour of the evening, he would not attempt
to enlarge upon the subject of what the American women had done for
their country's welfare during the late four years' struggle for Union and
freedom. They were to be seen at those places where sufferings were
worst, volunteering aid to the sufferers, and helping the wounded as best
they could. A large amount of money was supplied by the Sanitary Com-
mission, nine tenths of which was contributed by the female sex. What
had been the accounts that had been received with reference to the
conduct of the ladies during this long war? The answer was well
known. Wherever battles had taken place, the ladies had flocked to the
depots; had rendered everything that lay in their power, for the comfort
and happiness of the sufferers. Where would they find in the hour of
sickness and trouble consolation equal to that which woman could bestow?
They could safely say that during the war the ladies had done as much
for the country's sake as the men had, and encouragement had been given
by mothers and daughters to their sons and brothers, even in the shape of
friendly and hearty "good-bys" and parting inspirations, when leaving
their homes to fight for the cause of this great struggle—liberty. (Hear,
hear.) It was woman who followed man from the cradle to the grave, and
it was woman who consoled them in their direst despair. Would that he
had the eloquence to do her justice. He concluded by asking for the ad-
dition of these words to the toast: " Woman who carries all the graces
and the smiles of life." (Cheers.)

May he and his gentle wife be spared to return home in
the fulness of health ! And when he does return, we hope
the ladies of New York will succeed in charming the eloquent and generous merchant to "the stand," for the American who can speak well in London, must not be permitted
to be silent when dwelling at home !

July 25th, 1865.

MANHOOD SUFFRAGE.

TO THE EDITOR OF THE MORNING NEWS.

(*November 1st*, 1859.)

"Bitter jest that the most Civilized portion of the globe should be considered incapable of self-government."—DISRAELI'S *Cont. Fleming.*

SIR : Intelligent politicians will not be satisfied with less
than Manhood Suffrage. They believe that Manhood Suffrage is a Right, that it must be had before justice to the

toilers can be realized. They look with contempt upon the illogical subterfuges of their opponents. A deep-settled conviction has taken hold of the mind of the people upon the suffrage. Under existing political conditions, we have no chance of redress. M. P.'s may "beat about the bush" as much as they please, they cannot destroy the facts that abound.

We have more to dread from pretended friends than from our foes. "Respectable" gentlemen abound who don't like to go too far—who don't like to offend anybody. Rather than do so, they would let the millions continue at starvation's point. They do not dispute your statements, they admit your facts, they fully sympathize with you, yet they will not assist to remove the rubbish that obstructs general improvement. Political pendulums! They strive to be the advisers of Liberals and on good terms with the oppressors of humanity. It is too late in the day for such immoral proceedings ; we are not to be hood-winked any longer.

Professional men are obstinate impediments to political reform. Doctors do not like to interfere with politics lest they should offend some weekly purchaser of blue pill—some monthly sufferer from over-gorging. The lawyer constantly comes in contact with iniquity : among the rich he sees much dishonesty, intense immorality, and blind selfishness. He infers that the poor are infected to a greater degree. The inference is unsound. Comparatively speaking, there is less immorality among the poor than among the rich. Sturdy honesty is most frequently wedded to the greatest poverty. Witness such men as Andrew Marvel, Samuel Johnson, and the occasional finders of rich men's pocket-books, who are rewarded with a "Thank you."

It is said that asking for Manhood Suffrage is wanting more than can, just now, or even in a short time, be obtained. " Get a little at a time, is the policy of wise men." True, when the reverse would be impossible. But to change or inaugurate institutions you must change the convictions of men. To accomplish such, you must expend time, wealth, intellect, zeal, and continuity of effort. These must be

freely and constantly put into operation. Why not employ
such combination of forces upon a major, instead of a minor
object ? The cost is the same in either case. Similar
energy must be used—boldly, almost perpetually. For years
men have struggled for the Ballot, still it is far in the dis-
tance. Short Parliaments have long been considered an
important political necessity, still the subject is in the dis-
tance, and men have become tired of talking and writing
about the matter. These are minor topics, for good long
Parliaments could never be very inconvenient nor unjust to
the mass of the people, nor is the Ballot with an intelligent
people *absolutely* necessary. With all our agitation, we have
not obtained " a little" suffrage for working men. The political work has to be accomplished, despite of the enormous
" wind-bag " that has been emptied.

Change of opinion is a gradual result. Slowly does conviction of a permanent character arise. Hence, you can as
easily change the opinions of men upon major as upon minor
subjects ;—as easily up-root their prejudices against Manhood Suffrage as you can those respecting the Currency.
Therefore, let us strive for the major of political Reform—let
us work to obtain the power that will enable us to work out
financial regeneration. Doing so will be most profitable.
We shall be great gainers. Only one outlay of wealth, time,
and labor, would be required, for through the possession of
Manhood Suffrage, you have the mightiest impeacher of aristocratical imbecility.

The objection that the people would not know how to use
the suffrage is a piece of gratuitous impudence. How do
you know they " would not " until you have tried them ?
Recent historical facts settle the absurdity of the attempted
objection. In fact, under Manhood Suffrage, capital punishment was abolished in France. Here is a case of magna-
nimity exercised by the people—a case that cannot be paral-
leled in the history of priests and kings. The French people
declared the freedom of the Press, permitting knowledge to
be unshackled, expression of opinion to be "free as the soul
that dares to soar, free as the brain that dares to think."

Never have aristocratical governments manifested a similar love for thought and knowledge. The people adored God as revealed in books, reverenced the philosopher's researches and the poet's dreams.

Villains who had oppressed the poor, who had cheated industry, abused their power, degraded society, and who had enacted the basest laws, were unpunished—were not injured in the slightest respect by Republican France in '48. Clemency was exercised to the fullest extent. Contrast such conduct with that of our legislators, who for years would not permit a man, unanimously elected by a large and wealthy Constituency, to sit in the House of Commons, because he was a Jew. In a land that boasts of its freedom, a man's Rights are measured by his creed. Pagan Rome never adopted such disgraceful intolerance. Pagan Greece would have scorned the enacting of such injustice. A people is always more just than a sect, always more virtuous than a class. Manhood Suffrage is the father of liberty, and is the cause of national fraternity. In Italy, during '48, the people did not commit a base act—did not violate a single virtue, but extended the hand of mercy to the vilest members of the community.

> "Mercy droppeth like the gentle dew."

Print in letters of gold that " not a single condemnation to death was pronounced by the Republican government of Rome ; not a single one under the Republican flag of Venice." What monarchy can say the same ?* The purest intellect is ever democratic ; the most sacred national sympathies are always the result of domestic convictions. Despotism isolates, democracy fraternizes ; despotism restricts and destroys, democracy creates and extends. The first opens the " Valley of the Shadow of Death ;" the second sheds divine light.

---

* " Kings ! why, what's a king ? Why should one man break the equal sanctity of our race ? Is their blood purer than our own ?"—DISRAELI'S *Alroy*.

The further a nation recedes from democratic institutions, the more it has to "regret the past, distrust the present, and fear the future." At the present time "Paris is a comparative desert. No more life, no more animation, no more movement in pleasure or in business." The more freedom the more ease, comfort, peace and prosperity. A free people avoids tyrannous exactions, abolishes unjust restrictions, and diminishes or prevents extreme poverty. Business flourishes, commerce expands, intellect grows strong, inventive genius is stimulated. Generations arise from parental comfort, wisdom, and citizenship.

Despotism is the world's night, with no solitary star to beam and cheer ; no moon of love to cast around its lustrous beauty ; no warming sun of labor with force intense to warm and gladden the multitude. Under its deadening influence all hope is petrified, burning zeal and social emulation are cowed, and sympathy, struck from the rock of divine beneficence, becomes paralyzed with horror. Everything among the people becomes withered, everything among countries becomes tarnished. The poet's voice degenerates into a quaver, or else the harp is placed upon the wall, its notes of sweetness being for ever hushed. The philosopher stands silent before the objections of the priest and the commands of the King, or rather Emperor. The results of ardent investigations must be proclaimed to—nothing ; profound thoughts must be published to the mind that conceived them ; the fervor of youth is nipped by the frost of disappointment. Science is punished as a heresy, and Civilization is pronounced detrimental to the people's welfare. Vengeance is the law, cruelty is the administrator, brute force is the governor. We need not travel far for living illustrations ; need not search musty records for facts to prove—we have a demonstration across the water.

Governments of the very few are erected on huge pyramids of human bones, they are decorated with the groans of humanity, and guarded by the slaves of misery. Ignorance teaches, hunger drives, terror obeys. A deathly stillness reigns, and apathy drags its carcase through the abodes of men, regardless of consequences, and often frightened at its own haggard shadow.

The deliverer of the people from the thrall of power is Manhood Suffrage ; for it is the golden gates of the City of Freedom. Close the gates, not one single national wrong and abuse can be remedied ; open them, you can never traverse the blessed streets that will be revealed to you. Intellect presides over the City of Freedom and Plenty is the evangelist. Go to it ; be not turned from its gates. Listen not to deception clothed in "fine linen." Be not frightened from your object ; like Bunyan's Christian, resist the many temptations and allurements that surround you. Your dwelling-place is the mansion of co-operation ; your friends are knowledge, wisdom, and sympathy.

Leaving figurative language, let all Reformers unite to obtain Manhood Suffrage, so that every abuse can be banished from our land, and every institution that is necessary for the people's welfare can be created. Put every other question of home politics, at present, in abeyance. Petty details can be settled when our Rights have been won, when we have more leisure for trifles. Our work is to obtain, as speedily as possible, Manhood Suffrage. Financial Reform, even with the powerful assistance of Cobden and Bright, can make but little substantial progress as long as the majority of the people have no political voice, no power on the floor of St. Stephen's. As long as we are without Manhood Suffrage, aristocratical "noodleism" will drift us into wars, and prepare an effective Channel fleet *after* a sullen and treacherous ally has thrown his assassins (not soldiers) upon our shores, or sent his "floating slaughter-houses" to harass, in far-off seas, our commerce and our reputation. We must be constant, persistent, undeviating, unflinching, and utterly regardless of the whining cant of timid friends.

Yours, truly,

W. W. BROOM.

* PARK LANE, LIVERPOOL.

THE MAN OF DESTINY.

TO THE EDITOR OF THE MORNING NEWS.

(*September* 2*d*, 1859.)

" Le représente devait vous un principe, une cause, une défaite. Le
principe, c'est la souverainete du peuple—la causa elle de l'empire—la
défait, Waterloo."

"He hated, he persecuted, he crushed everything which had a tendency to excite the love of liberty."—J. A. St. John.

" There is a taint in his blood—he springs from a bad stock—he has
no sympathy with free institutions, no love for the people. All his lean-
ings are Dynastic, and by professing faith in Destiny, he has provided
himself beforehand with an excuse for any crimes he may commit. He
will always think it sufficient to attribute them to the overruling influence
of his star. Against such a man the citizens of a free country cannot be
too much on their guard."—J. A. St. John's *Life of Louis Napoleon.*

Sir, — Familiarity sometimes makes us intrusive. As
you were pleased on a former occasion to insert in your
columns a letter from my pen, I again intrude upon your
space. Once more, I hope I shall not be " rejected."

Just now, England is in alliance with a man who believes
in Destiny. Among all the monarchs who make freedom
tremble and humanity shudder, *only one* professes to act
under the guidance of a principle—of a principle as un-
changeable as are the laws of God. Russia, like old Rome,
dreams she will become an universal ruler, *in secret*—publicly, as in the late war, she pretends to wait, to watch, to be
directed, as circumstances indicate or determine. One power
proclaims that its base of action is a fixity—the other power
avers that its base of action shifts with circumstances. The
measure of one you can take once and for all ; the measure
of the other must be taken frequently—just as often as new
combinations of circumstances arise. The man of Destiny
must not be judged by what he has done (solely), is doing,
or what he *promises* shall be done : you must determine his
character by the object of his supposed Destiny.

The men of Destiny comprise two classes. One class believe that their Destiny will be realized, without the slightest

effort or interference on their part. They are the patient waiters on Providence, intensely firm in their convictions; seldom bad of heart; whose actions, being aimless, are not often vicious   The second class believe that they are *always* to watch and work to accomplish the Destiny that is Destined for them!—their logic we have naught to do with here.   To this class, judging by his words, writings, and actions, belongs Louis Napoleon, the mystic monarch of the shambles. To the second class (I shall no more allude to the first class in the remaining portion of this letter) Mahomet and Loyola were connected.   How antagonistic were the objects of their Destinies and results?   The Eastern mystic soddened the earth with human gore; the converted soldier went forth to sweeten the earth with the fragrance of Christianity.   Thus, we learn, the man of Destiny with a good heart, allied to profound thoughts, becomes a philanthropic hero, a national blessing: the man of Destiny with a *bad* heart, allied to egotistic crudities, charms with his promises the confiding, cheats with his solemn silence illogical minds, till, like a stealthy tiger, he becomes a destroying monster, not easily to be caught and chained.

Bulwer hints (in *Zanoni*) that believers in Destiny are not as potent nor as dangerous as generally supposed.   He, I think, makes a mistake.   All earnest men *are* potent, and dangerous when bad; and the believers in Destiny are the most earnest of earnest men.   Intensify a thought until you fancy or believe that the thought is to be made vital, by using the lives of other men, *for your sole benefit and glory:* how earnest, how potent, how dangerous you become!   Such, in miniature, is a correct, I think, description of the man of Destiny.

Let us apply the logical sequence to "the living present."

I repeat, we are to judge the man of Destiny by the supposed object involved in his Destiny.   His words and actions may or may not be, at the time, a logical development of his Destiny, but a mask to conceal his *real* development. To him all acts and subterfuges are justifiable; for he hears only one command, "Fulfil *your* Destiny"—reads only one sentence for his code of life, "Do anything to realize your Destiny"—sees only one honor, Destiny accomplished !

Louis Napoleon has always believed himself to be a man of Destiny ; born for one mission ; created to stamp his Destiny on thrones, on peoples. When a vagrant in London and New York, when gambling in "hells," when lounging "at Blessington's," when writing for a radical publisher, he always believed in Destiny.

And the object of his Destiny is the restoration of the Empire. What is the Empire ? Unrestrained freedom isolated in one man—that man is Napoleon—and slavery for *all* the rest of mankind.

What was the Empire founded by the first Napoleon ? Imprisonment, banishment, and death to opponents. The press only allowed to admire the character, to applaud the words, to adore the acts of *one man*. The existence and exercise of political and ecclesiastical power concentrated in one palace, by and for *one man*. The nation crippled, corrupted, subjugated—to prevent resistance, public spirit, and national volition. When the nation was crushed into a mass of slaves, then the *one man* turned his attention to the tearing-up geographical boundaries, so that the world should be *one* Empire—the Empire *one man* over a world of oppressed, chained humanity. Glorious Empire ! — one ray of life glimmering in a planet of death.

Such was the Empire ; it rested on a bar of steel, and was broken by a still heavier and longer bar of steel. The force that created became the destroyer of the Empire ; foul wrong crushed, and right made triumphant, in spite of Destiny encased in steel ! The Destiny of Louis Napoleon is to restore throughout the world the Empire of the first Napoleon. Ought we to rely on the words, implicitly, of a man with such an object fixed in his mind—ruling his life ?

Yours, truly,

W. W. BROOM.

ST. JAMES'S STREET, LIVERPOOL.

THE EMPIRE IN EXILE AND IN HARNESS.

TO THE EDITOR OF THE MORNING NEWS.

October 25, 1859.

" In a mitigated form, it has been one continued reign of terror. Any man's house may be entered at any moment, his most secret cabinets may be searched—his papers (even the letters of his wife and children, his marriage settlement, or the title-deeds to his estate) may be seized, sealed up, and carried for examination to the office of a commissary of police. Nothing is held sacred."—L. A. ST. JOHN's *Life of L. Napoleon.*

" I am now obliged to admit (whilst refusing to absolve crimes or forgive corruption) that the Empire succeeded to the Republic because the French nation mistook its aspiration towards liberty for liberty itself; and that NAPOLEON III. reigns by exactly the same right as other monarchs— by the tacit consent of a people adapted to his rule."—B. ST. JOHN's *Purple Tints.*

" Let Napoleon the Third become a free-trader, and all his crimes will be forgotten. * * * There is imminent danger that England may yet disgrace herself by a timid subservience to powers which will undermine or overthrow all her institutions the moment they are able. The English are too proud to fear this, or too ignorant; at any rate, there is moral mischief to themselves in their present position. Their forefathers bled for liberty and bequeathed it to them. They enjoy it, but have no longer to struggle for it."—M. PULSKY's *White, Red, Black, in* 1853.

SIR,—Despotism in its glory is brutal, in its decadence it is cowardly, in its fall it is contemptible. In its days of splendor it commands no respect, in its days of suffering it commands no sympathy. It is fawned upon by the timid, despised by the just, hated in the secret growls of vengeance by the poor. Placing itself *above* all law, human or Divine, it is feared when its claws are sharp, it is unpityingly crushed when its powers are almost spent. Isolated in its prime, it becomes doubly isolated in its dotage—isolated from its brutalizing ambition, from its bloody and plundering desires, from the world's care, and from God's approval. It is a huge mountain of ice, around which the dank, dark mists of death constantly gather.

The Empire in exile became a coward and a blackleg. Con-

fined to an island for a time, it fretted, fumed, bewailed. Its
days were devoted to gnashings of the teeth, its nights to absurd regrets. The dignity of silence, understood by the
philosopher and appreciated by the historian, was too majestic for the Empire. Noisy and bombastic Proclamations—
noisy and regretful lamentations—were the vulgar characteristics of the Empire in its power and in its powerlessness. The
Empire, baffled in its attempts for universal dominion, com-
plained of harsh treatment in the slang of cowards, and died
with a curse upon its lips and the love for assassination branded
on its heart. Thus the Empire was unworthy the historian's
pen, and only entitled to universal contempt. Soon men
ceased to contemplate the rotting carcase of a cowardly
butcher, and turned their attention and devoted their labor
to the building of freedom's altar on the ruins of despotism.

Resurrectionized in the dark, the Empire glided like a
stealthy burglar from place to place. It had no peace, and
wandered, like a doomed and troubled ghost in the midnight,
in the by-ways of the world. Shivering in the rags of past
glory, rags peeled from corruption, men passed with dis-
gust, contempt, avoidance, or forgetfulness. The Empire
wallowed in the lowest depths, without a golden crown to
dazzle, or imperial robes to conceal the revolting and destruc-
tive baseness of its nature. There was no repentance.
Troubles did not chasten the Empire in exile, nor soften with
purity its vileness, nor stem the torrent-tempest of its fiendish passions. It bid defiance to humanizing tendencies, and
dwelt in the gutters of corruption. It amused itself by
repeating in miniature the art of plundering, the acts of
tyranny, and sullen obduracy to public opinion.

In London and New York gambling-houses, it chuckled
over its fraudulent accumulations, as, in its day of glory, it
had chuckled over its triumphs of blood. It "bilked" its
creditors, leaving the hotel-keepers "between two days," just
as once before the Empire had "bilked" small potentates,
and deceived great nations. It became a "special" constable
to prevent the imagined existence of a revolutionary out-
break—being true to itself, it resisted opinions with the

bludgeon, when not able to use the sword. It sneered at the press, because the Press would not proclaim the existence of greatness when no greatness was manifested. The Empire would not or could not create a reputation out of noble deeds—it wanted a reputation made for it out of words—mere words. In exile it wanted to repose, as it always has reposed, on laurels grown and fashioned by other hands. The Empire is lazy, knavish, deceptive, and murderous ; these qualities were as strongly developed, under the circumstances, in exile, as they have been in the chair of Imperial power. The leopard cannot change its spots, nor thistles grow without sharp-pointed thorns, nor despotism without being base, brutal, and corrupting.

I have little space left to describe the Empire in Harness, and must leap over, with a passing sentence, how the Empire once more got in Harness.

France, full of faith and restlessness, fond of theories and blood, priestly regalia and Imperial shows—panting for conquest without expense, and perpetual glory without a shadow —glory sprinkled with sweetened water, and baptized with human blood—threw herself into the arms of the Empire, a second time, and has been well hugged. She joyously listened to words solemnly and oft-repeated, read proposed extirpating theories with *eclat*, and believed that the Empire that had dispelled the dreams of a ROBESPEIRRE and a CONDORCET would eternally cover with the flowers of Socialism the land of political stagnation. Some persons, we are told, never learn, and some nations never remember. But the Empire promised so finely, swore so well, went to church so regularly, never missed mass, nor forgot confession ! Poor France ! She has got to learn what the poet knows, that

" He who is ALL faith is NO faith at all."

Again, the Empire is in Harness, driving the chariot of Despotism. For ten years it has luxuriated with a nation's purse in its hand ; for ten years it has rioted with a nation's faith in its keeping ; for ten years it has lived holding the

sway of a nation's power ; for ten years it has cajoled a people—deceived great powers and tantalized small States.

Need the results be epitomized ?   Intellectual death, progress put back, war deified, successful villany sanctified by
vacillating traitors to the Cross, fair promises made to be a
mask for secret scoundrelism, slavery's chains covered with
rewards to cunning butchers and gambling financiers to conceal disgusting moral rust, the temples of knowledge, the
wings of publicity, the halls of justice, the tribunal of legis-
lation, the schools of philosophy, the instructional abodes for
youth, are all being converted into a Pandemonium to minister to the brutalizing gyrations of a monster.

Yours, truly,

W. W. BROOM.

PARK LANE, LIVERPOOL.

"DONE TO PERFECTION."

THE FIRST PART.

THE SPECTRE.

A Spectre flits from place to place. Nervous, irritable,
feverish—it is ever restless, and knows not the soothing gentleness of repose.   Cold, icy, selfish—it seeks to become an
all-powerful Reality !   Born in the dark region of despotism, nursed among political storms and dynastic convulsions,
it hates humanity, and would strike mankind with palsying
terror.   It represents an Empire without land and without
subjects—an Emperor without crown, without purple robes,
without a chair !   No home !   A miserable Spectre that
glides among the tents of strangers, unrecognized, unfeared.
Without a shirt, without a purse, after dismal wanderings—
succored by a woman's pitying heart.

Covered with the robes of pity—surrounded with the ele-
gancies of wealth—supported by Charity—still the Spectre
is grim, repulsive, devilish.   Not warmed, though in the
mansion of affection.   Not frank, though feasting at the
board of hospitality.   Not easy, though every comfort is an-
ticipated.   Generosity intensifies the Spectre's coldness,

gentleness deepens its feverish desire to "reign in hell." It gambles to learn skill, it prowls in gutters to study the wriggling power of "black worms." It smells the fumes of corruptions, and for a moment rejoices. It hears the howlings of "damned spirits," and for a day experiences a thrill of delight. It sniffs the air of a million battle-fields (with CÆSAR in the clouds), and swells in height and in bulk. The only music that can charm the Spectre is—the sighs, moans, and groans of the despised and oppressed.

But pity and charity dwelling in the heart of Beauty fed, and clothed, and housed this monstrous Spectre. O woe supreme for the nations! O dreary disappointment for affection! The Shadow is becoming a Substance—the Spectre is enlarging into Reality. It has cheated the poor, it will cheat the rich. It has visited "Socialists," but it will make an *extinction* of their hopes. Lodged in "the Tombs," it will make a gilded tomb for freedom, and grow "green" as it contemplates its genius. "It's only a Spectre!" mutter the half-terrified fools. "It's only an unfortunate Spectre made wretched by cruel adversity," apologetically breathes forth the sweet voice of dear woman's sympathizing nature. And while the people debate—the Spectre lives and moves, and *plots infamy*. It is "Done to Perfection!"

THE SECOND PART.

THE MURDERER.

Years have flown away, how many it is bootless to count. "Bilked" washerwomen have died. Abandoned democrats, socialists, old friends and mistresses have wandered into Oblivion. The haunts of politicians have been changed into "dancing saloons." As you peer into "Coger's Hall," fresh faces greet you with wondering eyes. Strange voices sound forth the rhetoric of study. Afar off, rumbling sounds are heard, lightning flashes across the valleys and twinkles above the tallest mountain-tops. The earth shakes, thrones totter, and monarchs are pale with fear. More noisily booms the thunder, more vividly flashes the lightning—and beneath, the lurid rays above and the dark earth below, a Spectre is

borne along on Death's pale horse. More violently totter
the thrones, livid become the monarchs' cheeks. Destruction is moving among governments, and chaos is revelling
among coronets. Amid all, the Spectre is riding to save
"society"—in time it will work to save CÆSAR !

Clearer is the atmosphere. The Spectre has been Deputy,
and is now President—*pour quoi!* The Spectre has sworn to
save "society" (always "society" is the slang pronounced)
and "liberty, equality, and fraternity." It is arranging to
fulfil its promise.

Smoke, and fire, and blood—society is saved, saved by the
Spectre that has communed with CÆSAR ! An oath has
been broken, justice has been derided and defied, the young
and the innocent have been MURDERED, philosophers and
patriots have been banished, dungeons have been filled—but
the Spectre has saved society !

Swing high the incense—chant boldly the harmonies—let
swords be rattled and muskets grounded—the Spectre sits in
a crimson room waiting to be crowned with Reality. The pale
horse now sleeps, Death has spread his pall over a nation's
sickness, no thunder booms, no lightning flashes—c'est
paix ! Was it not accomplished by the Spectre swiftly,
and "Done to Perfection" ?

The Spectre sleeps at last—and dreams. And here the
dream is mapped.—A woman's Spirit knelt beside the purple
bed, on finest carpet, beneath richest canopy. Crowns, and
sceptres, and a conquering sound (the sound of CÆSAR), and
a nation's revenues, shone upon the sleeper's sallow face. The
Spirit looked with mournful eyes. The beloved of pity and
of charity was the garotter of freedom, the murderer of national
conscience, and the breaker of a gentle woman's heart.
Around the kneeling Spirit appeared the souls of wronged
ones. Defrauded friends, orphaned children, deceived depu-
ties, defeated justice, outraged humanity, a bleeding generation
—a host of souls gathered around Heaven's kneeling Spirit,
once earth's joyous seraph. Still the sleeper slept soundly, for

he was under the "spell" inscribed upon a scroll held up at the sleeper's feet by the Phantom of Cæsar. But, in time, the kneeling Spirit rose, and as it turned from the sleeper to the Phantom, the souls departed and the sleeper woke; woke to hear a thousand, thousand curses hissing in his ears, and to see his gorgeous room filled with dancing and grinning fiends. He clutched the air, he writhed his body, he gasped for "liberty," and as he spoke, the Phantom approached and said—"Rise, take the pen, sit at the table, write *my history* (Cæsar's history !), then the fiends will depart, and for a little while you may have peace ; but let the work be Done to Perfection." Was the command fulfilled ? Was the promised peace obtained ? Or was it only and indeed a dream ?

THE THIRD PART.

THE SCRIBES.

In a splendid Cabinet a fidgety Scribe is giving peremptory orders to engineers, librarians, consuls, antiquarians, type-founders, and *prefets of police*. In a plain room, old and new books on a common table, newspapers on the old-fashioned chairs, a Student sits, contemplating his country's misfortunes. Orders given, contemplation ended, the Student becomes a Scribe, and the Scribes make notes and gather materials—one for Julius Cæsar, the other for Labienus. One Scribe writes to appease his fears and dispel the world's scorn ; the other Scribe writes to be the Nemesis of his country. The eyes of the first Scribe are furtive, canine-like ; the eyes of the second Scribe are bright, peering, and mild. The face of the first Scribe is dull and heavy as hate and crime can make a Felon's features ; the face of the second Scribe is bright and soft, beaming hope upon a nation's despondency. As the first Scribe writes, his heart is filled with fears, his mind with doubts. As the second Scribe writes, his heart is filled with joy, his mind with confidence. The first Scribe labors to produce a portentous *Apology* for *Crime ;* the second Scribe works to scarify a people's shame. While the first Scribes writes, the fiends watch and giggle ; while the second

6

Scribe writes, angels record the deeds of a good and bold man's life. While the Scribes are writing (unseen by both), an atmosphere from Gehenna gathers round the first, and fragrant airs from Heaven encompass the other. CÆSAR looks upon the one, CHRIST gazes upon the other.

The works of the Scribes are finished. The Spectre goes forth as a Scribe and declares that *he* is the Ghost of CÆSAR, and Labienus, in the garb of a Scribe, affirms that the Ghost is a mocking Fiend ! The world listens, hears both sides, and judges that Labienus is right. The verdict pronounced is— " The Spectre is a learned fool, a ponderous imbecile, made ponderous through Absolutism, made imbecile through villany !" Verily the work of the *second* Scribe was

" DONE TO PERFECTION !"

THE LANASHIRE DISTRESS DURING THE AMERI-CAN REBELLION.

LECTURE IN STEVENSON SQUARE.

Last night upwards of fifteen hundred people assembled in Stevenson Square for the purpose of hearing a lecture delivered by Mr. W. W. Broom, on the " Present condition of the operatives and shopkeepers of Lancashire." The lecturer spoke for an hour, and in that time passed in review the causes that led to the present crisis. He was of opinion that the war in America would last a considerable time longer. He urged that Parliament should assist in keeping the operatives now ; that the flow of liberality would not be sufficient to maintain the people out of employment until the crisis was passed ; and the Poor-Rates could not be increased under the present unequal distribution of the working of the law. Not less than two millions of money ought to be voted by Parliament. He intended carrying on the agitation in favor of a Parliamentary grant until it was made. The people, by a unanimous show of hands, expressed their desire shat the lecturer should continue the agitation. This meeting, which was quite orderly, is to be followed by others on the same subject in the same place.

The Manchester Examiner and Times, March 24th, 1863.

MEETING OF OPERATIVES IN STEVENSON SQUARE.

Last evening Mr. W. W. Broom addressed a meeting of operatives in Stevenson Square. The speaker announced that he would "propose a plan to the rate-payers that would save them from ruin, would rescue the unemployed from their present perilous condition of dependence upon precarious charity, and preserve Lancashire from physical prostration and the country from moral degradation." A cart was drawn up near the lamp-post in the centre of the Square, and about seven o'clock Mr. Broom made his appearance. There were about fifteen hundred persons present. In the course of a well-connected address, Mr. Broom urged the necessity of an immediate grant of at least two millions pounds sterling from the Consolidated Fund for the relief of the distressed, and contended that the Lancashire operatives were as much entitled to such a grant as the people of Ireland were to the grant of seven million pounds sterling during the period of the potato famine. The whole of England had, he said, been enriched by Lancashire, and in her nec. ssity the county ought to be supported by the nation. Much had been done by private charity and by the machinery of the Poor Law, but they could not expect a repetition of the splendid contributions which had been made, and the poorer class of rate-payers were becoming gradually impoverished. He would say to the Guardians of the poor, and to the rich men of the city, that if they did not fall in with his suggestion, and save the small shopkeepers from beggary, the riot at Stalybridge was but the sounding of the tocsin that would reverberate throughout the whole county. He did not wish to excite any prejudice against the Guardians or the Relief Committees, but he contended that both would be brought to a dead-lock, and that the only remedy for a national calamity was a national grant. At the conclusion of his address the speaker asked for an expression of opinion as to his sentiments, and received an almost unanimous vote of approval. A man named Fitton also addressed the meeting, which very quietly dispersed.

The Manchester Guardian, March 24th, 1863.

PROPOSED NATIONAL GRANT FOR LANCASHIRE.

Last evening Mr. W. W. Broom again addressed a large meeting of operatives in Stevenson Square, in advocacy of his proposal for a grant from the national Exchequer for the relief of the distress in the manufacturing districts. He said that by the middle of next June two millions and a half of money would be spent in feeding the unemployed operatives. There must, however, soon come a limit to private benevolence, and to the power of paying the Rates levied for the relief of the poor. The *Times* told them that if Lancashire was blotted out to-morrow, notwithstanding the 1,200,000 people usually employed, and the £8,000,000 floating wages fund, England would still be plump and healthy. It was cruel and insulting to talk in this way to people laboring under misfortunes over which they could have no control. The *Times* said that the people of Lancashire would degenerate into savages if they were well fed and had nothing to do, and evidently wanted to drive the people to rebellion. There would then be an argument against giving the people any increase of political power. He regretted that misguided boys should have acted so imprudently in Stalybridge and Ashton-under-Lyne. In robbing the co-operative stores they were actually robbing working men. The doers of these deeds were poor fellows who were goaded on by men who ought to know better. The working men of Lancashire who countenanced the preachers of violence were countenancing their own enemies. The behavior of the operatives in Preston and Blackburn, where the suffering was greatest, was a better test of the good feeling that existed, than fifty places like Stalybridge. The labor and wages of Lancashire had helped to enrich all other parts of England. In their distress, the people of Lancashire were entitled to ask for national assistance ; and he urged them to apply to the House of Commons on its re-assembling after Easter for a grant of £2,000,000 to feed the people until the return of employment. The speaker occupied the attention of the assembly for about an hour and a half, and at the termination of his address the meeting quietly dispersed.

The Manchester Guardian, March 31st, 1863.

PARLIAMENTARY GRANT ASSOCIATION.

Last evening, Mr. W. W. Broom again addressed a large meeting of operatives, in Stevenson Square, in advocacy of the proposed application to Parliament for a grant of £2,000,000, for the relief of the distress in the manufacturing districts. He stated that an Association had been formed for the purpose of agitating the question. Two meetings would be held in Manchester in the course of next week, and a Memorial would be sent round for the signatures of the rate-payers, asking the Mayor to convene a meeting of the inhabitants. Arrangements were, also, being made for holding meetings in Preston, Blackburn, Bolton, and other places, from all of which petitions would go up to the House of Commons, asking for a national grant. The meeting, after giving three cheers, as expressive of their agreement in the sentiments of the speaker, quietly dispersed.

The Manchester Examiner and Times.

MEETING IN STEVENSON SQUARE.

Last night, a meeting of the unemployed operatives was held in Stevenson Square, to receive a statement from the Deputation appointed to wait upon the Manchester Board of Guardians. Mr. W. W. Broom took the chair. Mr. Hart, one of the Deputation, said the guardians had received them courteously, and had referred them to the Mayor to endeavor to get the Public Works Act put in operation. A similar statement was made by Mr. Starkie, the other member of the Deputation, and he gave it as his opinion that the Guardians were not at all inclined to do anything more for them. The

Chairman then addressed the meeting. He blamed the rate-payers of Manchester for their inaction in this matter. They were very backward in paying the Poor-Rates. If they wished to decrease those Rates, they should compel the corporation to put the Public Works Act into operation. Those who had now to live upon the relief granted by the Guardians would then be enabled to subsist by labor. The unemployed ought not to be put to stone-breaking and oakum-picking, as such labor was only fit for criminals. When the Public Works Act was made operative, the men would earn more money, and be satisfied. It was ultimately decided that a Memorial should be prepared to urge the Mayor to carry out the Public Works Act in Manchester. A public meeting is to be called to adopt the Memorial.

The Manchester Examiner and Times, Aug. 22, 1863.

MEETING OF UNEMPLOYED OPERATIVES IN STEVENSON SQUARE.

A meeting of the unemployed operatives was held in Stevenson Square, last evening (Friday), to receive the report of the Deputation appointed to wait upon the Manchester Board of Guardians. Mr. W.✦W. Broom was called upon to preside. Mr. Hart, one of the Deputation, said the Guardians had received them courteously, but had referred them to the Mayor, to get the Public Works Act put into operation. Mr. Starkie, the other member of the Deputation, made a similar statement, and said the Guardians would do nothing for them.

Mr. W. W. Broom then delivered a long address, in the course of which he blamed the rate-payers of Manchester who were very backward in paying the Poor-Rates, for not compelling the corporation to put the Public Works Act into operation. If this was done, the Rates would be relieved, and those who were at present in receipt of relief, would be enabled to obtain an amount of pay for work which would serve to maintain them. As the unemployed were only unfortunate, and not criminals, they ought not to be put to the work

of criminals, stone-breaking and oakum-picking. They were
honest and unfortunate men who were being cruelly treated
at the present time. Let the Public Works Act be put into
operation ; they would earn more money, and would become
perfectly satisfied. Mr. Hart again addressed the meeting,
and said he had been surprised at the manner in which the
Guardians had treated their Memorial. He said the Guardians
reasoned that if they had starved the poor ten years ago, they
had a right to continue to do so. It was, in conclusion, decided to draw up a Memorial to the Mayor, urging that the
Public Works Act should be put into operation. A meeting
would be called to confirm this Memorial, prior to its presen-
tation to the Mayor.

The Manchester Courier, Aug. 22, 1863.

ADDRESS TO THE RATE-PAYERS OF LANCASHIRE.*

" The Central Executive Committee regret that the employment of workingmen in cotton mills and loom-sheds has again undergone a *considerable*
REDUCTION."

" What is to be done next, we really do not know. We perceive that
at a meeting of operatives held in Stevenson Square on Monday evening,
Mr. W. W. BROOM, in a remarkably temperate speech, urged the necessity
of an immediate grant of at least £2,000,000 from the Consolidated Fund,
contending that the Lancashire operatives are as much entitled to such a
grant as the people of Ireland were to the grant of £7,000,000 during the
period of the potato famine. Although there may be some doubt as to
the expediency of such a course, there is none as to its justice."—
Manchester Courier, March 28, 1863.

" The first point which is indisputable is, that funds will be forthcoming
in one shape or another, sufficient amply to meet the purpose ; and this
without laying any very grievous burden either on the county or the
nation. * * * But no one fancies that England or Lancashire cannot
maintain the unemployed operatives and those dependent upon them for
a year or two years if necessary, even although these should swell to
double their present number. Four or five millions, if properly levied
and adjusted, will not sink a ship like ours."—*The Economist.*

RATE-PAYERS !—The American war, that prevents Lancashire from obtaining a full supply of Cotton, is still raging

---

* This address was written by W. W. BROOM.

—the ranks of the unemployed are weekly on the increase—public charity has diminished from £35,000 to £5,000 per week—the Poor-Rate has been enormously increased, and is still being largely extended—and, at present, before you and the unemployed there is only a " dismal future." In many towns, some of you are unable to meet the excessive demands of the Guardians—nevertheless, the unemployed *must* be fed. Numbers of you who are now paying the heavy Rate will be unable to do so three months hence. As public charity lessens, the Poor-Rate will be increased—and you will be called on to pay, while your customers are disappearing, and your business is dwindling away. If you can't pay the enormous demand that the Guardians will have to make within the next six months, your " stock in trade" and household goods will be held in mortgage, or will be sold at far below their value, and you will have to be added to the mournful list of the unemployed. Such would be an accumulation of calamities disastrous to the nation and fearful to contemplate.

Until the American war terminates, your trade will remain paralyzed, and a multitude of operatives and others will be unable to *earn* the means necessary for life and health. *You* must not be ruined by the mighty effort that is being made to help those who cannot help themselves—nevertheless, the people must be fed and housed.

There is only one way of extrication from the huge difficulty—and the way is—a *Parliamentary Grant* of £2,000,-000 (at once) for the Cotton District. The principle was sanctioned by the late SIR ROBERT PEEL, and was successfully adopted for the people of Ireland in the time of their famine. Parliament adopted the principle of advancing money to distressed agriculturists many years ago. What was right in the case of Ireland cannot be wrong for Lancashire. The unemployed ought to be kept by the nation, not by a *portion* of the Rate-payers of one county. Lancashire has enriched the whole nation, and will again do so when her trade revives—hence, the nation is morally bound to contribute to her maintenance.

We earnestly urge you to join us, and subscribe to our funds to enable us successfully to agitate throughout Lancashire the necessity of an immediate Parliamentary Grant for the unemployed, and for the preventing of your ruin. Already Addresses have been delivered in the City of Manchester with marked success—the local and a part of the London press have favorably reported the Addresses. We desire to bring the subject before the attention of the House of Commons.

RATE-PAYERS !—be wise and be firm, unite to save yourselves from *Ruin*, firmly demand that the general taxation of the nation be devoted to keeping the unemployed until the Americans sheathe their swords, or until an adequate supply of Cotton can be obtained from other Cotton fields,—then our misfortunes will dissolve and disappear, like a cloud before the generous and majestic sun !

April 2d, 1863.
Committee-Rooms, 8, Port street, Manchester.

THE ANTI-SOUTHERN LECTURER.*

" Nothing would induce us to believe that Slavery was anything but a *foul blot* upon the Southern institutions."—LORD WHARNCLIFFE ; *Speech at the " Southern Soiree."*

" Was their cause (the Southerners') so just, was their success so manifest, that they were entitled to recognition ? Why, their cause, so far as he had been able to discover what it was, was not one to recommend itself to the sympathies of this country ; they had, apparently, by a wanton act, broken up the greatest empire which the modern world has seen. They

---

* These reports are copied from the English press, as matters of historical curiosity. They indicate the difficulties friends of the North had to undergo, and the contemptible way in which Northern advocates were reported. When facts could not be gainsaid, the proclaimer of the facts was maligned—when arguments could not be refuted, the arguer was imperfectly, incorrectly, or scarcely reported. When the advocate persisted in continuing his advocacy, intimidation and violence were resorted to, while *pretended* liberals looked coldly on. All that has passed away. The writer is satisfied with seeing the North victorious, and counts his struggles and sacrifices as one of the bright eras in his life.

were, so far as any MANIFESTOES they put forth were concerned, *wanton revolutionists.*"—MR. MASSEY, M. P.; *Speech in Salford, January 8th,* 1864.

" England would have been for ever infamous if, for the sake of her own interest, she had violated the law of nations, and made war in conjunction with the Slaveholding States of America, against the Federal States." —EARL RUSSELL ; *Speech at Blairgowrie.*

" Every *prominent* politician, and particularly those that belonged to that district of the country, had thrown the whole weight of their powers into the Northern scale."—J. M. COBBETT, M. P. ; *Speech at Oldham, January 28th,* 1864.

WE, the undersigned, have great pleasure in testifying to the talents, consistency, and zeal of W. W. Broom, on behalf of the Northern side of the American question. He spoke continuously on behalf of the North, *long before any society* was established in Lancashire. We gladly inform those gentlemen who are strangers to MR. BROOM, that any Subscriptions or Donations that he may solicit and obtain (or that may be solicited and obtained on his behalf by *authorized* persons), will be faithfully and honorably spent in counteracting the designs and influence of Southern agents.

J. C. LONG, 247 *Bradford Road, Manchester.*
T. CRABTREE, 2 *Tiverton Place, Ardwick.*
E. THOMAS, *Oak Bank, Sale Moor, Cheshire.*
F. CRABTREE, 92 *Lord Street, Southport.*
W. HIBBERT, 4 *Bank Terrace, Cheetham.*
A. CRABTREE, *Bank House, Openshaw.*
T. MORRIS, *Fetter Lane, Manchester.*
C. HADFIELD, *Radcliffe, near Bury.*
THOMAS BOSTOCK, 4 *Bond Street, Manchester.*

MARYPORT.

THE AMERICAN WAR.—The Liberals of Maryport engaged Mr. W. W. Broom to give two lectures on the American war, in the Athenæum. The chair each evening was judiciously filled by Mr. Collins. There were as many ladies as gentlemen present, who often testified their approval with great applause. The lectures were elaborate—being histor-

ical, political, and moral. He termed slaveholders " human
pirates sailing on the high seas of humanity, under the black
flag of moral desolation." At the close of the lectures the
following resolution was moved by Mr. Collins, seconded by
Mr. I. Fletcher, and unanimously passed :

" *Resolved*, That in the opinion of this meeting the English government
must continue to observe a strict Neutrality; but if, during the progress
of events, it is deemed desirable to express any opinion, the English people will give their sympathy for Freedom and not for Slavery—for the
American Union, and not for the destruction of that magnificent home of
our brave and industrious offspring."

Appropriate remarks were made by. Mr. Collins and Mr. I.
Fletcher. •

Carlisle Examiner, Dec. 2, 1862.

OVER DARWIN.

THE AMERICAN QUESTION AGAIN.—On Thursday evening a meeting was held in the Assembly room, when Mr.
Broom, of Manchester, addressed the meeting, and criticised
the writings of Joseph Barker. At some length he noticed
Mr. Barker's very frequent change of opinions, and stated that
Mr. Barker was not a man to rely upon, and wrote and taught
according to the pay he received. Mr. J. Knowles Fish very
warmly replied to Mr. Broom, and stated that Mr. Barker
would again shortly be in Darwin. Mr. Fish became somewhat excited, and spoke with vehemence. Mr. J. Beckett,
who presided, had much difficulty in maintaining order. A
vote of thanks to Mr. Broom and the chairman terminated
the proceedings.

Preston Guardian, Aug. 29, 1863.

THE WRITINGS AND LECTURES OF JOSEPH BARKER.

On Tuesday evening, Mr. W. W. Broom delivered an address in the Temperance Hall, Hyde, " in reply to the writings and lectures of Mr. Joseph Barker on the ' *American
War—the whole question explained ;*' the character, falsehoods, fallacies, and insults of this apostate to the cause of

freedom, exposed ; the imbecility of this pompous and false prophet and slaveholders' advocate proved from his own *Review;* the effects of slavery and freedom, the duty of Lancashire, and the doings of the North clearly stated by impartial witnesses." Mr. Willis Knowles occupied the chair, and briefly introduced

MR. BROOM, who opened his discourse by defining the course he intended to pursue—to show that Mr. Barker was an inconsistent man, and that he would utterly deny the instincts of his heart, would utterly falsify the sympathies of his own soul for the purpose of enriching his own pocket. Before entering fully into the question he would give a specimen or two of Mr. Barker's inconsistency. Some time ago they had a meeting in the Free-Trade Hall, Manchester, and it was well known that Joseph Barker received money to go and destroy the liberties of that meeting. The two following nights Mr. Barker was announced to deliver two addresses in the Corn Exchange, but was prevented from doing so, because the people would not listen to him. The first night Mr. Barker sat on the platform a long time, and to pass time away, ate his supper before the eyes of his audience. The meeting dispersed without hearing Mr. Barker ; and the second night was as unsuccessful as the first. He (Mr. Broom) made it his business to be present before the chair was taken, and the whole of the audience were in the streets again at a quarter past eight o'clock, with him (Mr. Broom) at their head, on their way to hold an opposition meeting in another part of the city. On looking over the pages of his *Review* a fortnight after, it was found that at those meetings resolutions were put and carried by overwhelming majorities. Again, only a few weeks ago, Mr. Barker was lecturing in the Unitarian School-room, Newton Heath, when the chair was occupied by a gentleman who had voted that Mr. Barker should have the use of the room. Mr. Luke Pollard rose to move a resolution, when Joseph Barker objected, saying "I will not allow you to speak ; I have taken this room ; the room is mine." The chairman refused to put the motion, being afraid of displeasing Mr. Barker. However, it was put to the meeting in defiance of the chairman, not a single hand being held up against it. It has been said in the Hyde newspaper, that wherever Mr. Barker went he carried resolutions. Well, Joseph Barker went to Southport, and although one of the richest men in Southport was in the chair, the audience did not number more than sixty persons, the majority of whom were Northerners. At the end of the lecture, a vote of thanks was proposed to the lecturer. An amendment was made that Mr. Barker should receive the thanks of the meeting when he had *proved* the statements he had made to be true. The amendment was carried. When Mr. Broom's friend, Mr. Cooper, wished to say a few words, he was told he might ask a question, but not make a speech. Was that fair and honorable discussion ? At the commencement of the war it was stated that the Rebellion would be subdued in ninety days, and when Joseph Barker had a chance he would crack a joke over this prophecy ; in fact it was the only thing he could make a joke of. He would show them what sort of a prophet Joseph was. In his *Review* of the 14th of December, 1861, he predicted that " it is all but certain that in less than thirty days the Northern States of America, and England will be at war." On January the 18th, 1862, he wrote, " There is now no further prospect of a war between America and England ;" therefore, when Joseph Barker ridiculed Northern prophets, he should remember his own false prophecy. At the present time Joseph Barker was very pious. He (Mr. Broom) was not ridiculing *true* piety, but they knew how quickly Joseph Barker's features changed when he was depicting with sublime pathos the sufferings endured by the people of this neighborhood, during this horrible and dreadful war. It was a dreadful war, no doubt, but no one heard Joseph Barker lift up his voice against the Crimean war ; no one heard him speak of the sacrifices then made without a single political object being accomplished. The lecturer then entered at length into the American question, contrasting the writings of Mr. Barker, which he denounced as wilful misrepresentations when first written, or that he was

guilty of telling falsehoods now. We are sorry our space
will not allow us to continue our report, as the lecture was
a most instructive and eloquent one.

At the close of the address, discussions being allowed, Mr.
Kenyon made a few pithy observations on the American question, which were replied to by the lecturer, and the meeting
terminated peaceably.

The North Cheshire Herald, Sept. 26, 1863.

STOCKPORT.

On Tuesday evening Mr. Broom was announced to deliver
an address in the Northern interest, at the Oddfellows' Hall,
Stockport. The room was well filled, but Mr. Broom was
unable to proceed with his address, in consequence of the
uproar caused by the audience.

Manchester Guardian, Oct. 29, 1863.

A similar notice to the above (of the same date) appeared
in the *Manchester Courier*.

PUBLIC MEETING ON THE AMERICAN WAR.—An amusing
scene was enacted at the Oddfellows' Hall on Tuesday evening, on the occasion of a lecture being delivered, or, rather,
attempted to be delivered, by Mr. W .W. Broom, of Manchester, in " reply to the speeches and letters of Mr. T. B. Kershaw, and the lecture of the Rev. E. A. Verity." The hall
was far from being filled, but the audience manifested no
particular Northern proclivities. At the time appointed, the
lecturer made his appearance on the platform, and after a
brief pause proceeded with his address, dispensing with the
usual formality of appointing a chairman. The audience,
however, did not seem disposed to pass over the omission, and
interrupted the speaker with frequent calls to " Get a chairman," &c., mingled with certain mysterious allusions to the
antecedents of the lecturer, intelligible only to those who were
in the secret. In vain the lecturer tried to get " on" his subject, and no sooner did he mention the name of T. B. Kershaw than he was met with a round of cheers, and informed

" Kershaw's th' mon we want ;" others, somewhat curious, asked—" Who sent thee here ?" while others again, apparently anxious for his welfare, kindly admonished him to " Go whoam." At last, to the infinite delight of the audience, the lecturer resumed his seat, saying that if they wanted ten minutes' rest he would give it them. The opportunity was not unimproved by the meeting, a great part of whom began to chant the elastic American ditty of " John Brown's Body," with a rattling chorus of " Glory Hallelujah." The noise having a little subsided, the lecturer once more rose and complimented his hearers upon their musical abilities. He assured them that he would listen to them if they would not listen to him. He also told them that he was of "a most amiable disposition," and that " it would take a great deal to ruffle his temper," but the next minute proved the weakness of human nature by getting into a passion and pouring out a volley of choice epithets which we cannot sully our columns with by repeating. This, of course, rendered " confusion worse confounded," and at last the lecturer " packed up" his papers and hastily left the room amidst mingled cheers and groans. An attempt was afterwards made to continue the meeting in one of the lower rooms of the Hall, but the Southern element again proved too strong, and the idea was abandoned.

The Stockport and Cheshire County News, October 31st, 1863.

THE AMERICAN WAR.—The internecine contest now unfortunately raging between the Federals and Confederates in America seems to be furnishing pabulum for all the hired spouters in the country, if they can make anything by the *spec.* A person with Northern proclivities, calling himself W. W. Broom, a pseudo-writer about slavery, from Manchester, came over to the Oddfellows' Hall on Tuesday night, to riddle the letters and speeches of Mr. T. B. Kershaw and Rev. Dr. Verity, made in this town in defence of the South. The price of admission was one penny, and a companion named Cowell collected money at the entrance door. Mr. Broom's antecedents having arrived in town before that in-

dividual was enabled to reach the Hall, a pretty sprinkling
of Southern sympathizers hastened to get possession of good
places.   There was a fair muster of hearers, but in the end
Broom was not permitted to open his philippic ; and notwithstanding the gravity which his spectacles gave him, and
the animated appeals for order, not a syllable could be heard
touching either Mr. Kershaw or the Doctor of Divinity.
The scene on the platform from the end of the room was a
sort of pantomime ; there was plenty of gesticulation, such
as moving of arm, heads, and legs, but not a word could be
heard.   The contagion spread into the body of the room, and
here and there were knots engaged in animated disputations,
which lasted near an hour.   This made " confusion worse
confounded," in the midst of which, the peripatetic lecturer
and his friend managed to escape—pennies and all—and
speedily these Northern spirits were on their way, per rail, to
Manchester.   The only distinct voices in the meeting were
those who clamored for the return of the money ; and because they could not get it, or see any sign of it, they turned
round and " ratted" those who justified the visit of the fugitive lecturer, " or any other man."   The Police were frequently sent for to preserve order, but the fragmentary meeting eventually adjourned from the Hall to the room below,
where certain patriotic Yankee speakers were treated un-
ceremoniously.   The porter at length contrived to clear the
building and close the doors ; but a few lessons on North
and South fisticuffs were given outside, though with no other
result than a hint from the Northerners that they will soon
be straight with their opponents for stopping the legitimate
proceedings of this meeting.

The Stockport Advertiser, October 31st, 1863.

FREE SPEECH PREVENTED BY THE SOUTH-ERNERS.

To the Editor of the Stockport and Cheshire County News:

Sir : Yesterday I visited Stockport to deliver an address
in the Oddfellows' Hall, in reply to the speeches and letters

of the Rev. E. A. Verity and T. B. Kershaw. Before reaching the Hall, I was informed that a party had been organized to prevent me speaking, and to inflict personal violence upon me. At the time announced, I appeared on the platform, and commenced my address by informing the audience that it was my constant practice to allow any person, at the close of my address, to ask any questions, and to reply, if they chose, to my statements ; therefore, I requested a calm and patient hearing. In five minutes it was evident that the organized party was present, I was not allowed to proceed, and, after making three efforts, I dissolved the meeting.

I left the platform and entered the ante-room to receive and settle accounts. While talking to a few friends, the door was burst open, and the room was immediately filled with the organized mob. During nearly two hours I was "blockaded" by the ruffians of Stockport. At last, with difficulty, two persons managed to leave the room, to take a message from me to the Police Office, stating that my life was in danger. The police were sent, and, under their protection, I was escorted to a friend's house.

Thus, in your town, the courtesy due to a stranger was not awarded me—the privileges of an Englishman were denied me—the rights of a Citizen were destroyed—the laws of our land were broken—honest men, who had paid their money, were not allowed to receive my address—calm and grave deliberation in public on questions involving the welfare, progress, and freedom of humanity, was prevented by an organized conspiracy against public morality, free speech, and fair play.

How long will the people of Stockport submit to Southern despotism ?

Yours, respectfully,

W. W. Broom.

Salford, *October* 27, 1863.

This letter has been freely posted on the walls of Manchester and other places, with the following note appended :

7

" The above letter appeared in the *Stockport and Cheshire County News*, and in the *North Cheshire Herald*, of October 31st, 1863. The friends of FREE SPEECH, who are the stern opponents of organized ruffianism and Southern despotism, are requested to place this placard on the walls in the towns they inhabit. Working Men ! Resist the enemies of freedom, the foes of commercial enterprise, the obstacles to manufacturing industry, and the haters of Well-Paid FREE laborers. Do not allow free speech and public deliberation to be garotted by the sympathizers with Slave-mongers ; do not permit Slave-mongers to drive their blood-stained car over the ruins of Christian Civilization. No longer have the Heavens darkened with the Black banner of men-stealers ; nor have the mountains startled from their majestic repose by the hideous exulting shout of the receivers of stolen men, seduced women, and kidnapped children."

MR. BROOM'S LECTURE.

Last Tuesday evening, Mr. W. W. Broom gave a lecture in the Temperance Hall, George street, which was announced by a couple of placards distributed through the town, one of which set forth that the lecturer would criticise the writings of Mr. Joseph Barker and Mr. T. B. Kershaw, and the other was addressed to the people of Hyde, as follows :

" People of Hyde ! For the sake of truth and justice, for the sake of your dignity as subjects of a great and glorious nation, for the sake of universal Civilization, it is necessary that you should have ' correct information on the American question.' You should, if possible, understand the *objects*, comprehend the *views*, ascertain the *movements* of the Southern Independence Association. To assist you in the difficult task, Mr. W. W. Broom will read the Prospectus of the Southerners of Hyde, on Tuesday evening, Nov. 3, 1863, in the Temperance Hall, George street, Hyde. He will point out its morality—its grammar—its political economy —its confusion—its ignorance—its peace principle—and its selfishness."

Mr. WILLIS KNOWLES was appointed chairman, and briefly introduced the lecturer, who said he felt somewhat pleased in being present that night, because on a former occasion when he visited Hyde he obtained a fair, patient, and a candid hearing, and this had been the case wherever he had gone, save and except the previous Tuesday evening at Stockport, where the lovers of progress and the admirers of freedom had conspired together to prevent him speaking ! Before he arrived at the place where he was to lecture, he had heard of the conspiracy, and was therefore aware there would be no lecture. For two hours he was blockaded, and at last he was compelled to call in the assistance of the police, as he had stated in a letter addressed to the editor of the Hyde paper. That letter he intended to have reprinted and posted on the walls of Lancashire, so that it might be known by the working men the influence that was brought to bear by the Southern sympathizers in this country. Before proceeding with his lecture, he would read a Challenge to some of the chiefs of the Southern cause in England. He then read as follows :

A CHALLENGE TO BERESFORD HOPE, ESQ., JAMES SPENCE, ESQ., AND THE REV. E. A. VERITY :

GENTLEMEN : As you are the Advocates for, and the Representatives of, the interests of the Southern Confederate States —as you are trying to persuade the English people to Sympathize with the Southern Secessionists, and are trying to induce our Government to Recognize the Southern Confederate States—I thus publicly Challenge each one of you to meet me in public, to discuss, in London, or in Manchester, or in Leeds, or in Newcastle-upon-Tyne, the following propositions :

1st. That Slavery is the *only cause* of the Secession of the Southern States, and that the Southern Confederate States are being baptized in blood, for the purpose of maintaining and extending Slavery.

2d. That to Recognize a Confederacy that is based on Slavery, for the purpose of extending Slavery, would be a *crime* against the progress of man, and blasphemy against God.

I will undertake to prove the affirmative of these propositions, leaving to each one of you the task of negativing and disproving them.

Gentlemen—If you sincerely believe that you are on the right side—if you zealously believe that your opinions are sound—you will not be ashamed to have with me a " free and open encounter" before the people of England.

Hopefully inviting your acceptance of this public Challenge,

I remain, gentlemen, yours respectfully,

W. W. BROOM.

Salford, Nov. 3d, 1863.

That Challenge he intended to have printed and posted on the walls of Manchester and neighborhood next week. The lecturer then analyzed the Prospectus issued by the Southern Association, and declared that he would cheerfully meet any of the gentlemen named in the Challenge to discuss the subject referred to, but he disdained to meet such a man as Mr. Kershaw. The lecturer then alluded to the conduct of Mr. Kershaw at the Mechanics' Institution last week, when he attempted to palm upon his hearers a spurious document. At the conclusion of the lecture, the meeting was thrown open for discussion, but no person availing himself of the opportunity given, Mr. Broom made a few more observations, in which he made some very grave charges against Mr. Kershaw. Votes of thanks to the lecturer and chairman concluded the proceedings.

North Cheshire Herald, Nov. 7th, 1863.

MIDDLETON.

THE AMERICAN WAR.—On Monday evening a lecture was delivered in the Temperance Hall, on the fallacies and

falsehoods of Mr. J. Barker with respect to the American
war. The lecturer was Mr. Broom, of Manchester ; and the
address consisted of extracts read from Mr. Barker's recent
publications on the civil war in America, which were con-
trasted in order to show their inconsistency and consequent
unworthiness. Mr. Broom spoke about two hours, and was
repeatedly applauded. At the close, a vote of thanks was
passed to him.

Rochdale Observer, Oct. 10, 1863.

THE AMERICAN WAR AND MR. JOSEPH BARKER.

On Monday evening last a lecture was delivered in the
Temperance Hall, Middleton, by Mr. W. W. Broom, of Manchester, on the above subjects. The lecturer, on rising to
address the audience, began by observing that some time ago
he read in one of the Oldham papers a very long account of
the state of feeling in Middleton upon the American question.
It was an account which made one imagine they were all a
set of gladiators in this neighborhood, so strong was the
feeling. It went on to say that families had become
unsettled, friends separated, and he came to the conclusion that they were in a state of disorder. Judging from
the audience that night, he imagined that the inces-
sant rain had made many afraid to turn out, and that
their courage was cooled. Since he had entered the
town that evening, he had ascertained that some of the
Southern gentlemen had manifested their great love of public
investigation, and full public inquiry, in some cases, by destroying the placards placed on the walls. A placard was to
have been read in the Hall, but some one of Southern proclivities had destroyed it. A placard exhibited in a certain
place in town had met with a similar fate. After the above
remarks, Mr. Broom said they had to do that evening with a
gentleman of the Southern Club, who had been sent out, as
it was said, for the instruction of the people, but he (Mr.
Broom) would show them for the purpose of *misleading* the
people. One known not only in the manufacturing districts,

not only in the midland counties, but in all the counties of
England, as a man possessing influence on theological and
other questions.　One who had been retained by the Southern
sympathizers as one of their champions.　Mr. Broom said
there were certain qualities which a man should have when
he intended to appear before the public.　In the first place,
he should be consistent, and secondly, when a false statement
was made, he should be able to recognize it, so that he might
be prepared to advocate and defend his opinions in season and .
out of season ; but whatever might be the consequences—
whether poverty or riches ; whatever might be the opinions
of the public in contradistinction to his own, a man should
be firm in the principles he enunciated.　The speaker then
charged Mr. Barker with having wilfully and malignantly
proclaimed falsehoods for the sake of obtaining money ; and
with publishing and causing to be published erroneous reports
of his proceedings at the various places where he had been
lecturing.　Mr. Broom read an extract from a statement of
Mr. Barker's which said, " that the negro was treated as
badly in the North as South—was not allowed to vote," etc.,
whereas in the States of Vermont, Massachusetts, Rhode
Island, and Maine, the negro was allowed a vote, not only
upon local matters but upon other questions concerning his
interests, without any property qualification.　In the State
of New York the negro had a vote if he possessed a small
amount of property.　Another statement of Mr. Barker's
was, " That the Old Republican Party had declared that they
had neither the intention nor the wish to give the negro his
liberty."　When and where did the Republican Party say
this ?　It was incorrect.　After referring to the Fugitive
Slave Law, Mr. Broom said that the Republican Party was
formed in 1852.　Before the commencement of the war Mr.
Barker prophesied, " That the North would never conquer
the South," and was continually ridiculing the old " ninety
days."　In 1861 he said, " That in less than thirty days the
Northern States and England would be at war."　And in
January, 1862, " There is now no further prospect of a war
between America and England," so that when Joseph Barker

took upon himself to prophesy, he ought to have remembered that those who live in glass houses should not throw stones. He was *then* playing one card.   At the beginning of the war the Southerners were going to thrash the Northerners. Mr. Barker *must* have been talking with the senators at Montgomery, and they had told him that there was plenty of cotton—but they did not say where it was—and that if Lancashire could not get it, she would turn out in a general *melee*. He (Mr. Broom) might say that with all the contrivances in support of the South, in the shape of ships for the Emperor of China, Gregory's Pills from Scotland, etc., Slavery was doomed.   It was Vicksburgh to-day, Chattanooga the day following, and so on, until *all* the South would be conquered by the Federal arms.   Joseph Barker was *now* playing another card—appealing to the feelings of the men and women of England—denouncing " This cruel war—this barbarous war—this war of subjugation by the North.   Never was there the same number of orphans made ; never was there such a war in the days of the Roses, and Puritans." War was horrible, they knew, but there was a time in the history of nations when matters had to be settled by physical force, to destroy despotism.   Mr. Barker says, " John Bright is a clever man, and has been delivering an address in Rochdale, but John Bright knows nothing about the American question."   So with Cairnes and Mill, but Joseph Barker had been to America, and knew all about it !   He said (once upon a time) the government of America was the best friend of the working man ; no dukes nor earls there, pensioned on the London docks ; no princesses nor kings ; no State Church, grinding the people and robbing them ; there the poor man could sit under his own vine and fig-tree.   Thus Mr. Barker wound his way into the hearts of the Working Classes of England.   Did he tell them to go to the South ?   No, for he said that " in the South there was despotism, tyranny, and immorality ; where a man was not allowed to express his individual opinions, but in the North there was honor." *Now* Mr. Barker said that he could go anywhere in the South, and lecture upon any subject, and that he had done so. Where did he go down South ? He went to New Orleans, and lectured upon slavery ; standing before French creoles and slaveholders, telling them " that he had re-considered the whole question (he was always re-considering questions), and that the Northern Abolitionists had misinformed him, for he had found that slavery was a very comfortable institution." Mr. Broom read extracts from *Barker's Review*. Mr. Pollard, the editor of the *Richmond Examiner*, and Colonel Schaffner said that because the Southerners were defeated in the elections, they resolved to secede. By a similarity he might say that Lord Palmerston had succeeded in gaining the ascendency at the elections, whereupon the Earl of Derby, who was the opposing candidate, would endeavor to divest him of his office, because of his success, by causing a tumult among the people. Mr. Lindsay had the impudence to say that the North was not "sincere." Mr. Roebuck had said that the North was the "greatest bully in the world." He (Mr. Broom) wondered how any man could have the audacity to denounce twenty millions of people. "The Southerners were determined that if they were not allowed to govern the country, they would at least govern themselves." So that it was quite evident that slavery was at the bottom, top, and middle of the war. Mr. Barker was fond of talking about duty, and advising working men to do it, and said that, viewed in the light of the Constitution, and in a rational light, the Southerners were only doing their duty. Was it the duty of Floyd to send arms down South from the arsenals in the North ? Was it right to rob the public Treasury, or fire upon Fort Sumter ? Was it right for them to proclaim that no cotton should come to England until the government either Recognised the South, or broke the blockade ? After quoting Mr. Barker's views on the duty of the North, in contradistinction to what he had previously said, and making extracts from *Barker's Review*, Mr. Broom eulogized Northern partisans, and said that the majority of those who were in favor of Southern slaveholders, were against the interests of working men. It was generally the Tory interest. The very paper in London that was for the South, had its correspondent "Manhattan" in New York, was the Tory *Herald*. The Manchester *Courier*, the Tory paper, had the folly to tell them that the North was almost *exhausted*. They should remember that America had been the home of poor Irishmen, who, not being able to succeed in this country, had been welcomed there, and had succeeded in gaining a comfortable livelihood. America was the home of a vast number of Germans and others, who had crossed the dancing Atlantic to flee from oppression and poverty in Europe. Yet there were men in this country trying to bury the free institutions of America in the very depths of oblivion. Virginia gave birth to Jefferson, one of the noblest men, and he, like Washington, bequeathed in his will that the slaves on his estate should be set free at his death. There was a certain entail on the property of Washington, but his noble wife acquiesced in her husband's decision. If the Southerners did not abolish slavery when cotton-growing was not extensively carried on, was it likely that they would do it now? South Carolina, the first State that seceded from the Union, was thoroughly honest in the Declaration she set forth as her reasons for seceding, and they must give her credit for that. She said that from the very commencement of the Federal Constitution it was intended to destroy slavery. That it was the general impression, at that time, that Slavery would cease to be. The people had gradually become imbued with Northern sentiments, by the medium of public meetings, periodicals, newspapers, etc. The weekly and daily *Tribune* penetrated the Southern States. They were over-mastered by the press, the pulpit, and by many States' laws. Such was South Carolina's Declaration. Mississippi followed, and not a single orator in the South has dared to say that Slavery *was not* the CAUSE of the civil war.—(Hear, hear.) Mr. Broom concluded by denouncing Mr. Barker, as the Judas of freedom, who had received the blood-money, and sold himself to the enemies of mankind.

Previous to resuming his seat, Mr. Broom said that his intention was to visit all the towns where Mr. Barker had been, to expose his fallacious reasoning, but when there was an insufficient attendance, he was obliged to canvass for private subscriptions to defray expenses. He was not in the pay of the Union and Emancipation Society, nor of any other body, but depended upon private assistance.

It was moved by Mr. Commissioner J. Hilton, seconded by Mr. Richard Holden, that a vote of thanks be presented to Mr. Broom, and the proceedings terminated about half-past nine.

Middleton Albion, Oct. 6, 1863.

CONFUTATION OF THE STATEMENTS OF MR. JOSEPH BARKER, ON THE AMERICAN WAR.

On Monday evening last, a lecture was delivered in the Temperance Hall ; the subject in reality being the heading above. Had it not been for a slight accident at the close of the lecture, the lecturer's name would not have been known, as it was not announced on the placard. There was no chairman, and the platform was occupied by the lecturer alone.

Prior to making any statement with regard to the lecture, it may be well to clear up a small error which either the lecturer or the correspondent of the *Oldham Times* has committed. Subsequently to the commencement of his lecture, Mr. Broom, for that was his name, said that he had read some time ago, in the *Oldham Times*, a lengthy article on the state of feeling in Middleton in regard to the American war. He said that article set forth that the feeling in Middleton was such that friends became estranged in consequence of the opposite views taken, and thought that either the article was in error, or the continued wet weather had "cooled the courage" of the Middleton people. It may be said that the article referred to was the result of careful observation, and of information received from reliable sources. That there *was* great excitement was evident from the groups of people discussing the *pros* and *cons* of the matter until midnight, and recommencing when the day broke. Scores of people can testify to the fact that blows were threatened. Indeed, our correspondent himself had to beat an ignominious retreat in order to escape a blow aimed at a prominent portion of his physiognomy. It is absolutely necessary to make these statements, —first, because the respectability of a newspaper rests, in the main, on the truthfulness of the articles it contains; and secondly, to show the real error which caused the failure of the meeting. The placards announcing the meeting were posted on the walls of the town at or near midnight, and they were of such a nature that the printer did not affix his name, neither was the name of the lecturer read thereon. It went on to say that a lecture would be delivered on the American war; " the whole question explained, in answer to the writings and lectures of J. Barker; the character, falsehoods, fallacies and insults of this apostate of freedom will be exposed; the imbecility of this pompous and false prophet and slaveholders' advocate will be proved from his *Review*," &c., &c. The lecturer made some complaints that some gentleman of Southern proclivities had torn down and defaced his bills. This may be true; but it is true that many gentlemen of Northern proclivities condemned the said bill as opposed to all forms of decency, and calculated to endanger the plans they have marked out for the preservation of unity in America, and for the emancipation of the slave; for whatever failings the people of Middleton may have with regard to this momentous question, they will at least see that their cause is advocated honestly; nor will they offer any undue advantage to either side however weak, or suffer one immoral action that may hurt the feelings of their antagonists. Any course short of fair dealing and legitimate argument on a subject of such vast importance, is such as their sensibility can never forget, and such as their self-respect can never forgive. Therefore, those sympathizing with the South would not countenance the meeting, and those of the North were ashamed to attend—hence the failure. It is certainly painful to make statements diametrically opposed to views held; but the truth must be told. Regarding the lecture, it showed that Mr. Broom confined himself chiefly to contrasting statements made by Mr. Barker one with the other. This was

the work of two hours, during which time Mr. Broom was
frequently applauded ; and, at the close of the lecture, the
thanks of the meeting were accorded to him.

Oldham Times.

W. W. BROOM'S REPLY TO JOSEPH BARKER.

On Monday and Tuesday evenings (July 6th and 7th,
1863), Mr. W. W. Broom, of Salford, delivered addresses in
the Co-operative Hall, Oldham, on the American question,
in answer to the *Writings and Lectures* of Mr. Joseph
Barker.   During the latter end of last week two or three
attractive placards were issued for the purpose of calling attention to the lectures, and on Monday a counter placard
was issued by the Southern Independence Association, calling
upon the friends of the South " not to attend the meeting."
The charge for admission was 1d. each, reserved seats 6d.
About 1,000 people attended on Monday night.   There was
no chairman.

The Lecturer, on rising, said : Several months ago there
was a great want felt, and the want originated thus :—In
the town of Liverpool there was a gentleman residing, and
that gentleman had become an agent for the Southern
Confederacy.   He had also indirectly on behalf of the
Southern Confederacy, or directly on behalf of the Southern
Confederacy, appointed an agent in the city of Manchester
as his coadjutor in the work they had to accomplish.   They
had to do two things—first, to raise cash (a very necessary
thing in our day), and next, they had to try and create an
opinion among our own countrymen in favor of the South.
Besides the cry of getting cotton, there have been other questions involved in this conflict now raging in the United
States, and the difficulty was this—they had two tasks to
perform ; so they required assistance, and cast about to obtain men who could both talk and write, in order that there
would be sufficient mental power either for the platform or
elsewhere in favor of the South.   Time wore on, but the

friends of freedom were not asleep. They had preceded the Southern gentleman in Liverpool in organizing their forces, and London and Manchester had set the example of organizing for the express purpose of teaching the untaught in this country regarding the true nature of American politics and American tendencies. The result was, the formation of a Union and Emancipation Society. Counter to this was formed—first the Southern Club, and subsequently its brother Society, under the title of " The Society for the Recognition of the Southern Confederacy." There are two or three facts worth noticing respecting these two Societies. I have had it from a gentleman, who has received it directly from Mr. T. B. Kershaw, that the Southern Club was founded for the rich Southern sympathizers ; but as it was necessary to have working men in their ranks, and as working men are not always deemed fit objects to sit side by side with the gentlemen in broadcloth, a Society for the Recognition of the Southern Confederacy was formed, which Society working men are to join, and their richer brethren are to join the Southern Club. (Laughter.) Moreover, the subscription to the latter is 2s. 6d., but to the former it is 1s. if you have got one, and if you have not, they will be glad to take your name gratis. After these Societies were formed, they required certain officials ; and, after a time, succeeded in getting them. They have got a clerk whose name is well known to you all, no doubt—that is Mortimer Grimshaw. (Hear, hear, and cries of " Shame.") Some of you know a little about Mortimer Grimshaw's connection with the Preston strike, and some of you know a little about his connection with the Bolton strike. He sold the Bolton strike for £100. He went to London to try and sell the Builders' strike. He went to Liverpool and received £5 to try and break up a meeting that was held in Stevenson Square (Manchester), on the day the Prince of Wales was married. Instead of returning to Manchester, he and his *pal* got drunk, spent all the money they had obtained *under false pretences*, while unpaid men did what Grimshaw had contracted to perform. He is the workman's enemy and the oppressor's tool. After the Club had got him, they wanted an advocate—a man who understood and could work upon the masses, and in process of time up sprang "Simon Pure," in the person of Joseph Barker. (Laughter.) I am not going to deal with Joseph's religious character, but shall deal simply with his teachings on the American question, and leave his theology, good, bad, or indifferent, as it may be, to the care of others. You know that Joseph is a man who has had a *broad* coat made of many pieces and many colors. Some of the pieces have been true blue, some have miserably faded, and others have had a color that it would require a double magnifying glass in the hands of a philosopher to say what color they were. (Loud laughter.) You will remember that Joseph went to America once upon a time, and took up the business of a farmer, but getting tired, he thought it necessary he should return to the Yorkshire hills and to your own Lancashire breezes. And when he came, what did he do? Did he deliver New Connection Sermons? No. Did he talk about the mercy of Christ? No. Did he talk about the necessity and importance of people looking after their own souls? No. What then did he tell you? That the United States of America was a paradise, and advised working men to go to the land of promise. Told them they could buy land cheap; that there were no kings, no princes, and no State Church to uphold. He also said, "You will remember working men, that some time ago I wrote a book about slavery, and all I wrote then is true; therefore, for God's sake, keep in the North; don't go to the South at all." (Cheers and laughter.) Well, many believed Joseph, clubbed their money, and accompanied him to the United States. But in course of time Joseph returned and wrote and talked on behalf of the North; *never* for the South. But now he has become a strong advocate for the Southern cause, and publishes a *Review*, in which he takes to himself much credit for his cleverness, and considers that *his* opinion ought to supersede that of John Bright, P. Cairns, and others on the American question, for the simple reason that he, *Joseph Barker, has been to America.* (Laughter.) This *Review* by

Joseph Barker, happens to be the whole of the Standard Literature possessed by the Southern sympathizers in England. (Loud laughter.) Now, as Barker considers this *literature* so clever, if its contents can be disproved by its author's own writings, we shall have accomplished our object. But before we do that, let me tell you another thing or two about Joseph. First, that he received money from the Southerners to go to the anti-slavery meeting recently held in the Free Trade Hall, Manchester, for the express purpose of trying to create a disturbance, and that he bound himself to do so. A member of the Southern Club, who had some little regard for himself and for the reputation of the party with which he was connected, met Joseph and said to him, " Mr. Barker, I would not try to disturb the meeting to-night ;" to which Joseph replied, " I am bound to disturb it." Yes, he had entered into a contract and received money for that very purpose. (Shame.) On the following Thursday and Friday nights, Joseph got up meetings in the Corn Exchange. The first night he stood from half past seven to ten and did not get five minutes' hearing, while on the Friday night it was a complete failure, and before half past eight the doors were closed, and from fourteen to fifteen hundred people were in the streets. Joseph had certain resolutions which he afterwards reported had been proposed, seconded, and carried at those meetings in the Corn Exchange. (Laughter.) But what will you think when I tell you that nobody proposed, nobody seconded any resolution, for the simple reason that nobody would have been listened to had they attempted to read them, so that it is impossible they could have been carried, and yet Joseph tells us they were carried by " overwhelming majorities." (Laughter.) The lecturer here adverted to another mistatement of facts on the part of Mr. Barker with respect to a meeting recently held at Farnworth, and observed that if the Southern Club could not succeed by stating the truth they had better shut up. If they were afraid of truth they would do well to get as many Joseph Barkers as possible ; but if they wanted truth, the sooner they got rid of such a Judas as Barker the better.

(Hear, hear, and applause.)   But I had forgot to tell you that the president, or chairman, of the Southern Club is a gentleman who has been a filibusterer.   Mr. Broom then sarcastically remarked that the Southern societies were so strong that no clergyman or dissenting minister would allow his name to be published in connection with them, neither had any catholic priest sprinkled them with holy water.   (Loud laughter.)   The cause of freedom has on its side men of the noblest stamp, who are not ashamed to have their names published as friends of the North, including the Hon. and Rev. Baptist Noel, Dr. Guthrie, John Bright, J. S. Mill, Rev. G. Gilfillan, Rev. N. Hall, and others.   (Hear, hear, and applause.)   And I (said the lecturer) stand here to-night in a Representative capacity (as the representative of the convictions and sympathies of honest working men) and not as the agent of any society.   Upon coming here to-night I was told that it had been pretty freely circulated that I was here as the representative of a particular society, but I have to tell you that if there is any loss upon this night's meeting it comes out of my own pocket.   (A voice : " And the gain into your pocket."   Laughter.)   Yes, the gain into my own pocket, and I hope there will be one.   (Cheers.)   I rely upon the gratitude of the people, for in Manchester they raised me a £5 note by subscription, with which money I have taken this Hall ; and although we have not the room full to-night, I intend coming to Oldham again, ere long, for the Oldhamites appear to have been sleeping in this matter.   (Confusion.) Although the Southern Association in Oldham can boast of a few names, its agent is a broken-down schoolmaster.   (A voice : " And a drunken one too.")   He tried to be a respectable bookseller, but failed in that because of his own badness.   Reverting to Mr. Barker's writings, the speaker quoted from *Barker's Review* for Saturday, December 14, 1861, in which this sentence occurs :—" It is all but certain that in less than thirty days the Northern States will be at war with England."   Now let us take Joseph in his *Review* for Saturday, January 18, 1862, where he says, " There is no further prospects of a war between England and America."   (Laughter.) Therefore, when Joseph laughs at other false prophets, he should not forget that he once attempted to prophecy. (Hear, hear.) Hear what he says in another place. "It is probable, however, that the results (of the war) will be beneficial in the end so far as England is concerned. By cutting off our usual supply (of cotton) from the Southern States, it is causing our colonies to give themselves to the production of cotton, and it is probable we shall never again be dependent on America for cotton to so great an extent as we have been. In this case there will be little lost to the world at large." And so this man discovered that the war would be a blessing to our country, and would cause us not to be dependent on the slaveholders for cotton. Yet he is now going about and telling us that England and France, and other parts of the continent, will be almost ruined if we don't recognize the South. (Laughter and applause.) I pity that man who, after growing grey in the cause of freedom, sells his reputation for money, as Joseph has done, for a few weeks before he became the agent of the Southern Club he offered his services to the Northern party. Such a man is so utterly worthless that I don't intend to discuss with him, but I intend to follow him and undo what he has done. (Loud cheers.) He names three causes for secession, the first of which is the last election of a President. Mr. Barker is always telling that President Lincoln had an unconstitutional majority ; but Mr. Pollard, the editor of the *Richmond Examiner*, says that Mr. Davis is an unconstitutional President, and if Mr. Lincoln is so because Mr. Barker says so, then Mr. Davis is an unconstitutional President because Mr. Pollard says so. (Laughter.) Well, Mr. Barker tells us that the South seceded because the North had an unconstitutional majority, so that if the North had had a constitutional majority the South, I suppose, would not have seceded. But listen to another reason which Joseph gives for the secession : "One thing, therefore, which predisposed the Southerners to secede was, that they had no great liking for the Northeners and the Northeners had no great liking for them." Therefore, this great war is purely the result of the South not liking the

North and the North not liking the South. (Hear, hear, and laughter.) Hear another reason: "They (the Southerners) had no confidence in the justice and generosity of the Northern party, but believed that the Republicanism of the North meant that they were pledged to violate their rights and sacrifice their interests whenever it might suit them to do so." So that before President Lincoln is in office, the South know all about what *he* is going to do, hence the South secedes. Let us turn to Joseph again. In one number of his *Review*, printed in 1861, he says: "They (the Southerners) thought that the Anti-Slavery party was fast gaining power, and that their favorite institution (I suppose you know what this favorite institution is) was in serious danger." It is not cotton here; it is not tariffs; but it *is* SLAVERY. "Meanwhile," he says, "the Anti-Slavery movement was rapidly gaining ground, and when the election came, the Republicans gained a victory." A little while ago he said the North had an unconstitutional majority; now, he says, the North gained a victory.

After reading another quotation from Mr. Barker's *Review*, some confusion took place on account of Mr. William Halliwell, pawnbroker, Greenacres Hill, who at intervals threw out some jeering remarks to the speaker, which caused several parties to request his speedy ejectment. He still maintained his seat in the body of the room, amid the most deafening cries of "Turn him out! Turn him out!" The lecturer inquired who he was, and on being informed he was a pawnbroker, observed, "He knows that freedom for working men would be a bad thing for his shop. He knows that the pawnbroker lives out of the vices of society, the same as the slaveholder living out of slavery. (Hear, hear.) Pawnbrokers and publicans generally go hand in hand—the former get hold of your goods, and the latter of your money." (Loud laughter.)

Mr. Halliwell being unable to stand this, mounted the platform, and in a state of the greatest excitement essayed to address the meeting, but failed to get any further than "He has assailed my private character—(a voice: "Thou hast no character to defend")—and I come here to defend myself." (Loud cries of "Turn him out ! Pull him down !" &c.), during which the majority of the audience were standing, and evidently ready to take hold of Halliwell, and forcibly dismount him.

Halliwell now softened down a little, and said he would sit down when he had asked the lecturer two questions. The first was, " Were not the clothing you wear subscribed for by the Northern party ?" The second question related to the lecturer having placarded Manchester, but in the confusion that existed we did not get the wording of it.

At this stage of the proceedings Mr. William Marcroft was appointed chairman for the remainder of the evening, and as soon as order had been restored, the lecturer said : " I have just been informed that Halliwell is the son of a town councillor. If so, I am glad his father is not here, to see what a blackguard the son is making of himself. I hope the father will have some control over the madness of his son ; for a young man must be a madman that will rise up and disturb a meeting because the opinions expressed don't meet with his views. Never talk again of your ' Oldham roughheads,' for the only disturber of the meeting to-night is a *respectable middle-class man.*" (Applause and laughter.) The lecturer then went on to examine the writings of Mr. Barker, and at the close, the following Resolution was proposed and carried :

" That as the professed object of the so-styled Confederate States is the perpetuation and extension of slavery, this meeting declares its cordial sympathy with the emancipation policy of the United States Government."

SECOND LECTURE.

Mr. Broom delivered his second lecture, as announced, on Tuesday evening.

The lecturer prefaced his lecture by a few remarks on the report which had gone abroad in Oldham as to his being sent by some society. His reply to that charge was, that he should be happy to receive subscriptions to make up the loss of

some £4 which these meetings would be to him. He also
referred to a placard that had been issued by the Southern
party, calling upon the people not to attend the lectures.
He considered that was a proof that the recent victory gained in Tommy-field was but of a temporary and superficial
character, or they would not be afraid of the public opinion
being reversed by his addresses. Adverting to the public
meeting in Tommy-field, he said the speech of Mr. Steeple
was one tissue of falsehoods, and so complicated that it
would take him a whole night to unravel it. He then announced that the Society for the Recognition of the Confederate States were in want of a secretary, so that if there
was any young man in Oldham who had a character to lose
he might get rid of it advantageously by accepting that
situation. His own opinion as to Recognition was, that if
we recognized the South, without doing anything else, we
shall be laughed at ; and if we recognize it by breaking
the Blockade, we shall have a war with the North. After
talking for about an hour on general matters in connection
with this question, he at length came to his subject—namely,
Joseph Barker. Joseph had told them, in a recent work on
Recognition, that he " did not know what were other people's
thoughts on that matter." Well, if after three thousand
books on the subject had been published in the Northern
States, and nearly that number in this country, and yet
Joseph does not know what other people think about the
matter—Joseph had better sit down and read some of those
books before he begins to write for the edification of the people on the subject. (Hear, hear, and laughter.) But he
goes on to say, " The war has caused a depression in your
trade, the result of which is that I have seen in your streets
—(now mark what he says here, and I wish this place were
filled with the women of Oldham, that they could hear what
Joseph says of them)—I have seen (he says) more demoral-
ization, more vulgarity, and, above all, more indecency in
our streets than ever I witnessed before." According to
Joseph, the war has caused you to be more vulgar, more immoral, and more indecent than you were before the war.

Why, there never was a time when a greater amount of morality existed in Lancashire, or a more general respect to superiors and love of order than at present; and your patience is well known. Mr. Barker tells you further, that "something should be done for the people of Lancashire, not in the way of charity though." But in 1861 this same person writes, " The people of England ought to subscribe to keep the people of Lancashire." (Laughter.) Now I say, and always have said, that the people ought to be kept out of the Taxation of the country. (Hear, hear, and applause.) Again Joseph says : " Men are driven to emigrate." It would be a blessing if Joseph were driven to emigrate. (Laughter.) The nation would then get rid of a hired liar and a hired impostor. (Loud applause.) He is worse than the Judas of old, for *he* received the blood money and then hanged himself; but I am afraid Joseph will not do the latter deed. (Loud laughter.) Again Joseph tells you that " The North is waging a horrible war, a most cruel war." In reply to this, the lecturer read extracts from *The Iron Furnace*, and *Pictures of the War*, showing how the South conducted the war. Mr. Barker asks, " Cannot something be done in the case of this war, inasmuch as the North can never conquer the South ?" Well, the North don't want to conquer the South. The North wants to prevent Southern slaveholders from extending SLAVERY. But listen to a proposition by Joseph : "Might not England and France *demand* a cessation of hostilities, telling the belligerents they have fought long enough ?" Just catch a man and his wife ceasing to quarrel because somebody told them " they've done enough." (Laughter.) The wife would just turn on her heel and say, " Let us alone, if you please." Joseph says that " Justice, mercy, and Christianity, seem to require a mediation, and the world would not only justify, but applaud the act." Yes, the world—that is, Joseph Barker, Mr. J. L. Quarmby (of Oldham), T. B. Kershaw (Manchester), and Mortimer Grimshaw—" would applaud the act." The lecturer then adverted to arguments used by Mr. Barker with regard to recogni-

zing the South, because we had recognized Russia and Turkey, which had slaves. Mr. Broom said : It is a very long
time since Russia had any slaves, though she had had serfs,
but they were widely different from slaves, for they could not
be sold from the land on which they were, and if ill used by
their master, the land might be sold to other parties. And
as to Turkey, Mr. Barker should remember that she was a
nation long before we were, so that if there was any recognition, it was Turkey who recognized England. (Hear, hear.)
In conclusion, the lecturer said he should work night after
night in order to disseminate true ideas on this question in
opposition to those put forth by the greatest of modern scoundrels, Joseph Barker. (Loud cheers.) He would come to
Oldham week after week, provided it was no loss to him, until he succeeded in gaining a greater victory for the North
than the one gained in Tommy-field for the South.

The meeting broke up about ten o'clock.

The above is a report that appeared in *The Oldham Times*.
In reprinting it, mistakes have been corrected, blunders ex-
punged, and quotations accurately worded. The mistakes of
the reporter were numerous, surprising, ridiculous, and in
some instances his sentences were imperfect. A complete
correction of the report would impose the task of re-writing
almost every sentence. The adoption of such a course would
altogether ignore the reporter. We have no desire to bury
the results of his labor. We are grateful to the *Oldham
Times* for its long though defective report. Nevertheless, we
strongly object to being reported as saying on the platform
words that we never uttered. We are prepared to be held
responsible (*legally* as well as morally) for the statements we
make with the tongue and the pen, but we will not be responsible for the blunders of reporters, nor for the vagaries of
printers. Two sentences referring to M. Grimshaw, we have
suppressed ; in their place we have inserted five sentences
that were *not* spoken in Oldham. The conduct of this inces-
sant dabbler in strikes cannot be too thoroughly nor too widely known among the working classes. Vulgar "loafers"

should be avoided by working men. Such catiffs should be spurned by wealthy men from their clubs.

W. W. Broom.

THE PRESIDENT'S NATIVE STATE.

Sir : One of your correspondents in last week's issue of your impartial paper, informs your readers that Illinois is " the President's (Lincoln's) native state." The statement is a blunder. Had he said that Illinois was the President's *adopted* state he would have approximated to " correct information."

The generation of the Lincolns commenced in Berks county, Pennsylvania—a portion migrated to Rockingham county, Virginia, where the father and grandfather of President Lincoln were born.

Lincoln's father, " even in childhood, was a wandering, laboring boy, grew up literally without education." In 1806 he was twenty-eight years old, and married one Nancy Hanks, in Kentucky—the mother of President Lincoln.

On the 12th of February, 1809, Abraham Lincoln was born, in Hardin (now the recently formed county of Lane), Kentucky. Kentucky, says Schaffner, " was originally Fincastle county, Virginia," and " it was admitted into the Union June 1st, 1792." But Illinois was not a state when Lincoln was born, not until 1818 was it admitted into the Union, long *after* the " hunting-ground" had reached its prime.

I hope the foregoing will be of service to the members of the Southern Independence Association, and to your readers in general.

Before concluding, I will briefly state there is no good Life of Lincoln. The English one is dear and disappointing ; the one by Bartlett, of New York, is inelegant in style, and clumsy in construction ; and Thayer's *Pioneer Boy and How he became a President*, recently published in Boston, is only fit to amuse children. Surely the materials for a good biog-

raphy of Lincoln must be abundant in America. Is there no
Plutarch in Boston, no Smiles in New York, who can nobly
tell the story of the heroic career of the Titan of the North?

Yours, respectfully,   W. W. BROOM.

SALFORD, *Nov. 8th*, 1863.

A LARGE stock of *the Standard Literature* of the
Southern sympathizers is still on hand. Great quantities
would be freely given away if people would ask for it at the
waste paper offices. While "a discerning public" is buying-
up the stock, the author is carefully preparing a *Key* to the
work, that will explain the contradictions, prove the falsehoods, and vindicate the slanders that are so numerous in
the Standard Literature. As the notes of editors are generally larger than the works they edit, the *Key* will be more
voluminous than *the Standard Literature*—its price, therefore, will be three pence!

MR. KERSHAW is energetically engaged in printing
another hand-bill. When published, the work can be obtained at all the hoardings in Stockport. In consequence of Mr.
MORTON's generosity, in having introduced Mr. KERSHAW to
the public (converting a non-entity into "a public man"),
Mr. KERSHAW intends to make a well-assorted selection of
his hand-bills and present them to Mr. MORTON, bound in—
calf's skin.

A TELEGRAM *via* Halifax announces that a million
bales of Cotton, from the Southern Slaveholders' Confederacy, are on their way to Liverpool, as part payment of the
Confederate Bonds.—A *later* telegram states that the vessels
containing the cotton will pass Holyhead the day after—the
Day of Judgment.

GREAT

AND

GRAVE QUESTIONS

FOR

AMERICAN POLITICIANS,

WITH A

Topic for America's Statesmen.

BY EBORACUS.

BOSTON:

WALKER, FULLER & CO., 245 WASHINGTON STREET.
A. WILLIAMS & CO., 100 WASHINGTON STREET.

CINCINNATI:
ROBERT CLARKE & CO., 55 WEST FOURTH STREET.

New York:
C. S. WESTCOTT & CO.'S UNION PRINTING-HOUSE,
No. 79 JOHN STREET.

1865.

IN PREPARATION:

LITTLE BITS

ON

MANY SUBJECTS,

FOR

EVERYBODY'S TASTES

AND

DESIRES.

———

BY W. W. BROOM.

www.ingramcontent.com/pod-product-compliance
Lightning Source LLC
Chambersburg PA
CBHW032013010726
47493CB00007B/2377